THE DETERMINIST

Copyright © 2021 by Gordon Long

All rights reserved. No part of this book may be reproduced in any manner whatsoever without written permission except in the case of brief quotations embodied in critical articles and reviews.

First Printing, 2021

 ISBN 978-1-7778229-1-0
eISBN 978-1-7778229-0-3

GORDON LONG

THE DETERMINIST

PART 1

CHAPTER 1

The ground was sandy and there were cars everywhere, parked on slopes, bumper to bumper. The Norfolk Island pine trees were strong enough that they wouldn't let the cars slip into the beach from atop their roots. A long stretch of beach, full of people, chaos. Another with waves that came up to our feet as we stepped down off the wooden walkway. There were more beaches I knew of - this peninsula was my universe.

We could not decide on which beach to settle on, Jack obviously wanted to impress his friends and, for some reason, so did I.

"There are more further down past the plane hangar" I whispered to Jack.

We started walking further into the peninsula, to the thinnest part where the water was on both sides.

Jack furrowed his brow, "how much further?"

I decided not to answer him as we were coming onto the opening of the field where the small airport was - not really an airport as much as it was a small runway and a hangar. Knowing that there were more beaches past this industrial enclave, I steered us on towards the area where there were more beaches to choose from.

Jack turned towards the hangar as we walked past. I followed him in. His two friends drifted towards the hangar too.

Three women stood behind a couch on the other end of the building. I recognized Megan, her long blond hair and her constant uneasiness. I was about to call out to her when I saw what they were standing over. There was a young woman on the couch in her early 20s. She had long black hair and was dressed all in white. Her face was purple and there were white plastic cords around her neck.

She was suffocating and the others seemed to not care. As I walked towards her, the three women moved away from behind the couch and towards Jack and his two friends. I started untangling the cords around her neck. Her hair was getting in my way. I finally unwrapped the cords and watched as she took a big gulping breath, and the purple hue in her face subsided.

She smiled at me.
She sat on the floor.
She propped herself up against the couch arm.
She opened her right hand, in it she had clenched empty balloons. They were all different colours.

"What are those for?" I said gently.

"The doctor gave them to me last night when I tried to die. I swallowed all my pills at once," she said quietly, still catching her breath, though she seemed calmer by the second.

"So you can pump your own stomach?" I was confused.

"No, so if I felt sad, I could look at balloons and feel happy again." Tears started coming from her eyes.

"Can you tell me a bit about yourself? My name is Gregory." I slumped down on the wall to be at eye level with her.

Jack started coming towards us and sat down too. He and I had a way of communicating to each other that we were not leaving this girl alone. We thought: she will try to die again if we leave her alone, and her friends and Jack's friends were already gone.

"Maybe if I have one of the balloons in my mouth and you blow it up it will go into my lungs," she said desperately. The hopeful tone she used was jilting to Jack and me.

I began to cry and held her hand.

We sat there leaning up on the couch for the rest of the day. I held her hand. She wanted to die, but she wouldn't do it with me there.

***

Zoom Calls with therapists are the new norm in 2020, and my therapist keeps changing the location in her house where she conducts the session. Last week it was in a window, she was far from the camera and there were plants and a bookcase. There was a lot to look at, and a lot to drink in. This week it is a blank white wall and she is wearing a loud necklace. She always has good fashion.

"I am just trying to get the idea of this beach area, and those friends of Jack's. Do you recognize them?" she leads.

"It's just as I said in the dream. A long peninsula that I know well. It kinda reminds me of a peninsula in Cuba I went to a few years ago on one of those all-inclusive things..."

"And who is Jack to you? You've described him before as a good and honest friend, right?" she asks.

"Yeah, Jack is a good close friend, who seems mostly content with everything and what he isn't content with he says 'this is fucked' then laughs"

"And you don't recognize his friends?" she asks.
"No, nope, just don't know who they are"

"And this Megan woman, who is she to you?" she asks.
"She is someone I worked with last year, she is young and had a side hustle in some an online beauty product, she hated working in the bar and treated it like a stepping stone. She was very image-focused from memory, very chic and money-focused. Nice enough, but it was just her show in her mind."

"So her friends you don't recognize either?" she asks.
"No, but they were very much like that too, you know?"

"So let's talk about this girl who wants to kill herself. So she tried the night before, once in front of you which you stopped, and has plans to do it again, but you are sitting with her, and she won't do it with you there, correct?" she asks.

"Correct"

"How did you feel that day before you went to sleep?" she asks.

"That day, I was thinking about how hard this has all been. I kind of hit a wall in the morning. I did a workout but it wasn't very effective. I visited my neighbour who had hurt his leg. I made lunch. I went for a walk. Then I met up with my boyfriend, we went for a walk. Came home and made some food... watched something stupid on Netflix.... Kinda just ended up in bed. Pretty normal lockdown day"

"Did you have any suicidal thoughts?" she asks.
"Well, no, I mean 'the call to the void' feeling creeps up, but it's not like I am ready to shake the mortal coil or anything"
"Ok just checking," she said with a small sigh and smile.

"Let's discuss the girl more. I think that is where this dream is pulling you, it's where the center of the emotion is. There is a focus on how calm this girl is while she discussed killing herself. What do you think that means to you?" she asks.
"I mean, yeah, I was distressed when I saw her. I think that my way of stepping in to stop her was the right thing to do. I think her friends that were standing above her just watching was a little fucked up... I don't know of many people that wouldn't stop to help her. I didn't do much that no one else wouldn't do."

"And how did you feel discussing her death plans with her?" she asks.
"I guess I was interested in how creatively she was attempting to die. I remember a few years ago, when I was with Robert and he was being constantly dismissive of me, I remember hating myself enough that I decided one night to imagine all the ways I could kill myself in that house we lived in. Imagine from the top floor, in the bathroom, swallowing all the pills in the medicine cabinet or hanging myself off the banister staircase with a towel. Jumping from the top floor banister over the railing, and falling

headfirst onto the foyer. Slitting my wrists in the kitchen with a knife and bleeding out. Going down into the basement and mixing chemicals to choke on and die. I never thought to swallow balloons though."

"I'm not sure I remember talking about these feelings back when you were going through that time," she says, looking mildly concerned.

"I remember going through all of those feelings and trying to decide what would be the easiest way to die. It's just hard to talk about, hard to admit in the moment."
I decided not to relive the night I actually tried.
I decided to stop talking, which is the opposite of the need for therapy.
I just did not want to talk about that day right now.

"Hmm, it really is a testament to how far you have come when you look back on all of those moments and made the decision to make your life better. Look at how far you have come" she says.

"Yeah," I passively replied.

***

When the session was over I said goodbye with a smile. After the meat of the emotional work was done we had mainly talked about the statistics of suicide. We talked about the pandemic and how it was affecting people.
As I closed my laptop down, I felt sad like I hadn't before. There had been a genuine attempt for suicide that day, followed by months of standing on train platforms on the way to work staring at the front of the incoming train, thinking, 'this is it, do

it' and pulling myself back into reality. I guess the sadness was needed.

Should it be ok to grieve the potential loss that I was going to incur on myself?

What would have happened to the people around me? My sister, my parents? My friends? I don't think anyone would ever forgive me.

If I believed in post-life sentience, I guess I wouldn't forgive myself either.

CHAPTER 2

Living with intention when no one is looking has been a new chore to endeavour.

What is the point of cleaning the dishes at night when you live alone?

What is the point of keeping the doorway clear of outside clothes when no one visits?

What is the point of setting a table for dinner when I eat alone?

The first time I cooked for my new boyfriend Joseph, I made a squash soup.

It was November, the season for manufacturing warmth. I had bought two butternuts at the market a few days before. I had onion jam and garlic honey prepped. I was confident that the foundations of my cooking techniques would shine through with such simple and delicious flavours.

We had walked to the St Lawrence market to buy St Urbain bagels (a true luxury), and these were to be the best accompaniment. Everything was in place for me to impress him.

It was a Sunday night, he was beautiful and I was hopeful.

THE DETERMINIST

He came into the kitchen as I was plating our meal.

I spooned out the soup, sprinkled on za'atar, pumpkin seeds, onion jam and finally drizzled on the garlic fermented honey.

The dish was perfect and casually suggestive.

"Would you do this for yourself if I wasn't here?" he asked me.

"Beautiful food is worth celebrating," I replied, exhaling as I spoke.

We sat down at my dark wood table, his dark eyes and features dancing in the impractically low light of my apartment. I felt a tension in myself.

"Did you put ginger in this?" he said.
"Yes, did you just get a big chunk of--"
Before I could finish speaking he was pulling out an unpureed, mangled hunk of ginger.

"Oh, shit..." I started to laugh and he smiled.

He placed the small chunk of ginger on the side of the plate as I giggled through the moment, thinking it was typical that this would happen to me. An impatient misstep. A great chef would strain their pureed soup before serving, and would probably not try to pull off a culinary masterpiece in 37 minutes. I am impatient. I am falling in love with this man after 3 weeks of dating. I am impatient.

I turn music on, which is going to transform this night into something to remember. Not for the usual reasons you would expect with gay men, but with two people who had a small breathless moment when they first met.

I still remember seeing him for the first time. I walked up behind him. He was wearing a silk-lined baseball style jacket, held up by his very well-built chest and arms, black skinny jeans and a pair of turquoise turtle shell glasses. The removal of his covid mask was relieving. I remember thinking that he was going to say "no thanks, but thanks...'

His cheekbones hold his face up like an apple, his full lips and almond eyes are undeniably the signature of true beauty.

We started walking, we got a coffee, we talked, we kept walking.

We found ourselves at the bottom of Yonge street, outside the Van Gogh exhibit.

We kept walking.

We had met at 2 pm near my home, and it was now 5 pm at the waterfront. We sat down talking. The setting sun made his brown skin look gold.

He grinned.

He asked to kiss me and before he could finish his sentence, I moved into him.

I don't believe in magic.

And now he is pulling a piece of uncooked, un-pureed ginger out of his mouth. I sigh and acknowledge my lot in life: to be the silver medal of the world, always missing that final step towards perfection. Then I remember, he is sitting in front of me. At least I have this.

After a post-dinner talk, he leaves and I turn on the functional lighting in my apartment.

My tea steeps as I wash the dishes in the sink.

I sit down on the couch to reflect on my tea. I ponder the evening and think about Joseph and the way the light catches his brown eyes.

***

I am standing in my home, but it's not my home. It is a new version of my home, where everything is just a little bit off-brand. There is a pot of soup on the stove and it is too sweet.

I start to prepare more ingredients on the chopping board and open the lid of the pot to add the ingredients, but I cannot even see the soup because of the steam rising from the boiling liquid.

There is a room off my kitchen that I have not seen before and it leads out onto a valley with a tall ridge that is covered in vibrant green grass.
I take my apron off.
I retrieve my shoes from the front door and walk back past the stove with the pot on it. The lid is starting to rattle.
In the valley, there are a few things to look at: a bluestone jutting out of the side of the hill and going halfway up, obviously where there was a landslide. Luckily I am good at jumping, I can jump almost three stories up, probably further, I am yet to fail and fall.
I bounce up to the ridge. All I can hear is the rattle of the soup pot. It must be echoing.

There is a small area to sit up here and I can see further down the valley, to where it ends and the terrain levels out.
The soup pot is whistling and the rattle has turned into a bucking noise, like a large bubble that keeps forming and popping.

I can see my apartment far down in the valley, it seems the longer I wait the further away it appears, yet the noise of the soup pot grows louder and louder. I'm not sure whether it is time to return. I know there is something more up here for me to look at. And it won't take long for me to get down.

I don't know what it is I am supposed to be waiting for, but I can hear the soup pot. It is making itself very aware to me.

It has not stopped rattling with its sense of urgency for days now. It is penetrating all of my senses - I hear it, I taste its sweet yet burnt smell, I see it glowing inside the window of my apartment, and I feel the vibration of it every time a bubble bursts. It is consuming my thoughts.

Finally the bluestone I am sitting on quivers with the release of another bubble of the soup pot.

It is time to leave.

I move down the side of the valley mountain in five steps.

I tremble towards my apartment bringing my arms closer to me.

I step inside the apartment and walk through the office into the room that is playing the role of my kitchen.

I see the pot, which now has a foot of orange and yellow glowing molten lava crusted on it.

As I move towards it, the pot starts to implode, literally crumbling into itself. The mushroom head of crusted lava sizzles back into the pot.

Now on my stove is a crumpled, spent soup pot with the ashen residue of what was a well-intentioned soup.

It was a simple base of the foundations of cooking. It was a soup.

***

I clicked on the session begin button. The screen uploaded and I could see my therapist smiling at me. She was dressed in all white. A large black necklace swang around her neck.

We discussed the week and I bought up my new growing fear of the pandemic. It was hard to articulate that almost 9 months into the shutdowns, and the presence of a confusing and potentially life-threatening virus, it was only now that I was feeling deeper anxiety.

"Do you think you are feeling this now because it has been building up over time?" she asks.

"I mean, I have had a present feeling of anxiety over it for a fair while now, these times are scary" I replied.

"It is a hard time. Missing friends, going places. It's a lot to move forward with, but you have your coping mechanisms in place, your zoom calls, you talk with your sister, your runs." she says.

"Yes, and it's all helping a lot, it's just, I guess it's silly but, learning how to date during this"

I finally stammered to the issue. What a complete fool I am for saying this when the death toll this morning was larger than it was last week and more people were getting ill, and I just wanted to take my boyfriend to a fun pub and listen to live music.

I could see her glancing up from her writing pad. Did she think of me what I thought of myself?

"Well given that you haven't really dated much, or spent time romantically with anyone since Robert, is a lot," she says.
"I thought I would be good at dating, I went on a few dates last winter, and a few first dates this summer while the patios were open. I just actually like this guy. It's frustrating not being able to have a night planned around something fun, like going to see a band together and watching his reaction... It's hard to get to know what he likes."

"Yes but remember you haven't dated anyone in 8 years" she gently reminds me.
"Yeah and when I first started dating Robert we would go to the pub and play pool. We would go on little adventures. Now all you can do is go for walks around closed neighbourhoods and to the market."

My god, I sound like an asshole. The case numbers are climbing higher than ever in Ontario, we just hit our first lockdown number and it looks like it will baseball-style get higher. People are dying, and I am whining about going to the pub.

"Let's look at this dream" she suggests.

"Yeah" I am relieved she changed the subject.

"So you're in your kitchen but it's not your kitchen, (that happens in dreams,) and this soup pot is boiling over" she clarifies.

"Yeah, it's weird, right? It was exactly like my kitchen and apartment, except for this door off the side of my office that led up a hill."

"Yes, but I want to talk about this soup pot. You added more things to it even though it was boiling over," she said.
"Well yeah, and it was rattling, it's a real soup pot that I own too. It felt weird using it this week. I watched it implode in my dream and wondered if it would in reality as well."

"So you had this soup on the stove, you could feel it and sense it the whole time, and you knew when it was bubbling over. You also went up a mountain in a few steps. Did you recognize the mountain at all?" she wondered.
"No, but I have had adventures in mountain ranges before."

"Could you tell me where these mountains could have been? Were there trees? Was it snowy? Were there animals?" she wanted every detail.

"No, it was just a series of grassy hills that led up to bluestone ridges on the sides of mountains. I don't think I have been there, but when I was little I went with my family and my mom's friend to the Blue Mountains in Australia. I guess they kind of looked like that." I replied.

"Ok, so the mountains are more of a retreat from the kitchen. So this soup pot has lava coming out of it by the end?" she asks.

"Yes, and then when I returned to the kitchen it stopped cooking like the heat had been turned off, but I didn't turn it off. The whole thing just kind of imploded, it pulled itself into itself... I could walk close to it, but couldn't feel the heat from it. It felt important that I observed it."

"Would it make sense that this soup pot represents the feelings of anxiety that you are feeling and that maybe you are aware of them but let them boil along..." she suggested.
"I mean yeah, that does make sense..."

"Maybe the feeling of losing control during this time is giving you anxiety. You cannot go out too much, you cannot go to the gym. It's a hard time" she says.
"Well, at least I'm not sick with covid..."

"Yes, but it's normal to feel anxiety. You do not need to compare your feelings to the worst-case scenario" she reminds me.

"It just makes me feel stupid, all this death in the world and I am worried about the fact that I didn't puree a soup properly."

I felt tears coming up. I didn't want to cry in session. I could feel them working their way up my face, the hot feeling on the back of my head. My throat changed its position in my neck. Therapy should be an autopsy of past emotions not an onset of new ones.

"Gregory, are you ok?" she asked.
There was no holding this back.
"I just miss a lot of things. I miss things being easy and perfect and I miss the life I had. If I could tell myself five years ago where

I am today, I wouldn't want any of it. I wouldn't believe any of it. Imagine going back to twenty-five-year-old me, in love with someone, travelling, running marathons and working in a job I loved. I would have told thirty-year-old me to go fuck himself."

I wish I hadn't sworn at her.

She breathed in and looked satisfied. Was this response what she wanted from me?

I wiped my nose on my sleeve. I moved my glass of water around on the table out of the view of the camera.

"Sorry for swearing. I just got a little overwhelmed"

***

I closed the laptop down. Towards the end of the session, after taking a few moments to catch myself, we talked about the virus again, and she kept the session going for an extra ten minutes to make sure I was ok.

What I had failed to convey in that session was that I was falling in love with Joseph. That I was excited, even if our relationship was short-lived, that I could feel like this again. I thought this feeling had died a long time ago.

I poured myself a cup of tea, craving something stronger.

I sat sniffling on my couch, reading a magazine. My phone buzzed. It was Joseph.
"Do you still want to go for a run tonight?" he asked me.

How relieving.

CHAPTER 3

Joseph and I had made plans to spend the day together out walking to different neighbourhoods. The sun was out and it was frigid but bright. We met my friend Rose and walked around Kensington market in the cold. It was their first time meeting. I could tell Joseph was nervous, but Rose has never been nervous before.

We did what had become regular during the lockdowns: we picked up coffees and went walking, trying to stay out of breathing range while we sipped. Rose and I led the conversation by talking about a tragic character we used to work with. We all laughed and commented empathetically about our pitiful colleague.

When the sun went down, we said goodbye to Rose and walked back to my apartment, the temperature outside becoming unbearable. Joseph was shivering, and I put my scarf around his neck.

We shuffled through the front door into the warmth and shed our winter clothes. I ran my hands under warm water in the kitchen for a minute before I realized I was being inhospitable.

I turned off the tap and walked into my bedroom to find Joseph kneeling on my bed, looking out my window.

The view from my bedroom window is of neatly laid out townhouses set before a taller apartment building. There is a colourful mural on the high-rise to the right, and when the sun rises it is all I see.

At night time it is a beautiful sight. All the apartments light up and people wind their days down and go about their end-of-day rituals. Around thirty different dwellings, all with different tastes and decors, that I get a glimpse of. Some people have low lighting with a large TV lighting up the room. Some homes look warmer, with focused lighting designed to feature the art on their walls. One home has had Christmas lights up all year. I guess this is the year for it.

Looking out the window has become a way of feeling less alone. People have their rituals that I can observe casually from across the way. In my living room, I have a big blue wall with many little plants on dark wooden shelves. In my bedroom, I have a large tapestry of wildflowers with bees that looks tasteful in the right light. My bed is up against the window so that I can look out onto the twinkling lights of the tall buildings at night and the bright colours of the mural in the morning.

When I am alone at night the view feels comforting, and when I have company it is my private escape. I can drift out of the room and across the townhouses to someone else's living room, into their lives, and look at their things. But it is different when Joseph is here. He was sitting on the bed, quietly gazing out the window with his back facing me as I crawled over beside him.

In the bookshelf beside my bed is a roughly stacked pile of novels, biographies, self-help guides and a few notebooks. He looked at them all.

"Are you reading all of those at once?"

"I need to be in the mood to read some of those... So I just have a few different ones on the go at once... and those are journals."

"You keep a journal?" he seemed surprised, or maybe impressed, or maybe just inquisitive.

"Keeping a journal has been a habit in one way or another since I was a teenager. I wrote in small notebooks, kept paper calendars of events with annotations, I even had a written travel blog at one time." I said to Joseph.

He looked like I had just told him a secret. I continued.

"The information in them varies. For instance, I can tell you exactly what I had for breakfast in Israel ten years ago, also what time I needed to be at work five years ago. All my tax information was in there from the years I spent as a bartender, as well as some of my innermost secrets. It's like a strange little tapestry of profound thoughts weaved through the monotony of daily life, all written into little books."

He still looked at me as if I was giving up too much of myself.

"Here, look."

I pulled out a work-related entry from 2014 that I knew would be safe.

"On June 19, I worked for ten and a half hours and made two hundred dollars in tips" I recited

"What do the other ones say?" he asked.

"Secrets…" I replied with a smirk and moved in to kiss him.

After we had warmed up with hot tea, Joseph left for the night and I sat on my bed, looking at my shelf of diaries. To the left of the shelf, there is one that sits tauntingly, like an enemy. It holds things I don't want to read again. I don't want to throw it out, but I do not want to read it again.

In one motion, I lean from my bed, snatch it from the bookcase and retreat to the other side of my bed.

It felt different than it felt the last time I held it.
It looked just like the others except for the '2019' on the front cover. The pages were worn up to the halfway point, reflecting how busy life got that year. It makes sense that it wasn't full with entries - after all, I stopped writing in September. Finding a way to write about that time felt impossible.

My hands ran along the spine of the plastic-covered book that looked like wood, the grain repeating itself every five inches or so in the soft, brown, plastic adhesive paper.

Why did I feel this nervous to open something that I created and knew the contents of?

Memories are weird. Once, I read in TIME magazine that memories are imperfect. The article claimed that you never remember the actual event that takes place in the memory, just the last time you remember remembering the event. So the memory becomes corrupted. Damaged. Altered. A blue shirt becomes green. Words become more or, in some cases less, convincing. A lover's eyes look bigger. Six months can disappear.

I open up the notebook. The handwriting is undeniably mine: loopy on the vowels, sharp on the consonants, words penned with urgency, trying to keep up with the speed of the thoughts that birth them. I thumb through the pages, my writing sometimes slanted. Sometimes messy.

The ribbon divider marked where I stopped writing. I fold back a page and read:

'September 6, 2019
Long time since I wrote in here.. Sorry 'bout it.
It has been a busy few weeks with ups and downs, more downs.
I am becoming more and more convinced that I may need to just move very far away from here. Alone, and just be alone for a while. Take stock of myself.

Fuck all this stuff man...

I don't even like sleeping in the same bed as Robert and I am becoming increasingly convinced that he will just throw his hands up soon and tell me to leave.

I won't fight him on it again.

I'll just tell him to leave...

I am so over pretty much every aspect of my life right now.

I need to go down to 4 days of work a week at Beskära, I need to work more at Maverick. The money is just fucking better...

I need to be more like 20 year old me
He was FEARLESS
He knew the meaning of quid pro quo, I do too much shit for free. Everyone has a strip of me for nothing.
I used to make myself the first factor in every decision. Do what I want, how I wanted.

Robert told me tonight that it is hard for him to be sexually attracted to someone fat and emotional.
I could strangle him.
I'm still wearing size 29-inch jeans for fuck sake, I am not fat. I'm just not young enough looking for him.

We are basically just angry roommates at this point.

He won't listen to me for anything or any reason.

He obviously is sleeping with a younger version of me, I just fucking know it, how sadly typical.

Maybe if I just talk to him."

I closed the book.

I couldn't read anymore.

Pulling myself slowly across the bed, I placed the book back on the shelf, between the calendar of 2019 and the diary of 2018.

Crying normally helps me fall asleep after something like this.

I just had a wonderful day with someone I am falling in love with.

I feel worlds apart from the person who wrote that.

***

"So I didn't get a dream email from you this week" my therapist states.
"No, I didn't have one"

I had, it was about Geena Davis with her blond hair from the movie 'The Long Kiss Goodnight.'. God only knows why I was dreaming about that.

"Well, let's have a chat and see what comes up," she says.
"Sure, it was an easy week. Well, as easy as they are in lockdown. I met up with Joseph on Sunday to go for a walk with my friend Rose. We walked around Kensington and the University area... it was nice. I did my workouts and went for a run, but it was really cold out this week..."
I wish she would jump in and stop me from rambling...
"And I talked to my sister, we giggled on the phone for a few hours which was good, we kind of have our own language..." Was she going to jump in now?
Normally leaving a space in a conversation is a good point for someone else to jump in, but no.
"I talked to my mum which was strange, she seems excited by Christmas coming up." I pause again.
Am I charged by the word 'Christmas'? Lots of people are.
"I opened up an old diary. Joseph was asking me about the books on my bookcase, so I told him what they were. After he left I opened up the bad one."

Why would I say that? I do not need to offer up anything. She's meant to probe me for triggers, I don't need to give them to her.

"What is the bad one?" She seems glad to have a focus point.
"The journal I kept before Robert left me," I replied.

"What did you read?" She continues.
"The last entry. it was pretty dark, and very clear that I was in a dark place."

"What were some of the things you wrote?" She asks.
"I wrote about how I was feeling like I needed to get away, and how I wasn't happy with Robert. That I felt like if he tried to leave me, I wouldn't fight it - I would just let it happen."

"How did you feel afterwards?" She asks.
"Confused. I mean, I had just spent a day with someone wonderful, and then came home and read about someone who broke my heart."

"It can be confusing. The brain is strange. Love is chemical, and it makes its pathways in the brain. When you fall in love with someone new, those love chemicals go down the same memory pathway as the last time you fell in love." She explains.
"I mean, I get that, but I don't understand why I would think about Robert when I am becoming more and more in love with Joseph. It has been over a year since I was even in that relationship, and even longer since I was happy in it... I just don't understand why it is like this. I just want to move on."

"It's ok to think about someone you loved. They still exist there, in the time you loved them." She says gently.

"Why is this so fucking hard?"

I wish I wasn't swearing at her again, it's been four times now.

"You're going to move on, you're going to fall in love with other people, your life still goes on. You are 30, you have a long life to live." She says.
"But what if I only get it right once? What if I had my shot and I blew it? What if I am just wasting Joseph's time?"

"Getting stuck on 'what ifs' is not very helpful…" she reminds me.
"I don't know, isn't it called a soulmate for a reason?" I cut her off…

"I think we both know that people are capable of a lot more than a soulmate Gregory. Life is long." She reassures me.
"I know."

The computer audio sputters and the screen freezes cruelly, right as I'm on the cusp of an emotional breakthrough.

The pending sign comes on.
My brain switches from emotional epiphany to technical problem-solving.

The screen repopulates with the surroundings of my therapist's home, and she looks frustrated.

"Can you hear me?" She says a little loudly.
"Yes, YES… can you hear me?"

"Oh, this thing…" She is annoyed now.

The audio recovers and I see her face moving, though pixelated.

"Can you hear me now?" She's back.
"Yes, I can."

She sits in silence. It must be my turn to talk.

"I understand that it's silly. I just do not want to feel heartbroken because of those love chemical pathways, every time I fall in love with someone new... What if Joseph is the last person I fall in love with? What if he is the one I am supposed to spend my days with? What if he is the one I have my happy little forever with? He is wonderful and smart and kind and beautiful. I am just so scared."

"Can you hear me?" There are still technical issues.

Her screen looks stagnant and pixelated again.

I don't want to repeat myself to her.

There are twenty-four minutes left in the session. I am already emotionally tired.

"Yes, I can hear you. I was just saying about how feeling heartbroken about someone you don't love anymore, while you are falling in love with someone else is confusing. I just do not understand how my brain can betray me that way"

I am becoming angry. I can't tell if she can hear me. I can't tell if she is responding. I am flailing in the wind with nothing pulling me back.

Then she speaks - she could hear me.

"It is not an easy road. Remember the first few weeks after you and Robert split up? You were trying too hard to make people happy. You slept with people you didn't want to. You tried to be happy while being single very quickly. But you were unhappy." She reminds me.

"I wasn't going to waste time. I wanted to date people. He already had a two-year headstart on me." I try to justify the rebound.

I sometimes feel in these sessions that I am not being heard. And that I cannot articulate myself.

***

I was frustrated by the end of the session. My brain is betraying me. I cannot honestly expect the feeling of falling in love and the feeling of being broken-hearted to just swirl around in my head like this, entwining and tricking me into comparisons and trips down memory lane. It's insanity.

I lay back down in bed and look at the bookcase again. That journal sits there taunting me. I know what happens in those blank pages. I didn't need to write it down.

CHAPTER 4

I was walking through cold empty streets. There were old pastel stucco apartment buildings all around me. This part of the city looked like most European cities but felt a lot colder. It was night time and I could see my breath in the air. I was walking down alleys and making my way through dimly lit side lanes. The street lamps were few and far between. I was wearing a black peacoat with the collar popped up under my chin. My hair was a large mane of curly ginger locks that swayed with each step I took on the uneven cobblestone laneways.

Reaching a doorway, I pressed on the buzzer and quickly returned my hand to the warmth of my pocket and moved from one foot to the other, waiting for the door to click open. It was so cold. The door clicked open and I entered the foyer, unbuttoning my coat to let the warm air in. I started to climb the staircase that was only lit by the streetlight outside, somehow knowing exactly where I was going. I arrived at the apartment door, suddenly very nervous, and softly knocked three times.

A slim young man with brown hair, round glasses and a black turtleneck sweater greeted me. He told me I was on time, marked something down on his clipboard, and muttered something into the headset he was wearing. We stood in the doorway for a moment as he listened to something in his earpiece. He whispered back into the headset, then turned to me and gestured for me to follow him. We walked down the apartment hallway, the floors creaking under our feet. The hallway was dimly lit, and further down I could see what looked like a kitchen, only lit by the streetlights outside.

As we continued down the hallway I could feel the nervous feeling arriving in me again, as the air became thicker. The mood of the space itself was changing around me.

We arrived at a thick wooden door. He tapped on the door twice with his index finger, paused and then opened it. He stood back to let me in and I entered, nervously.

The room was warm and inviting, the floors did not creak in here. Red drapes sealed the windows and the whole room glowed. There was gold trim on the wainscoting and crown mouldings. A modest but beautiful chandelier hung in the middle of the room. The air felt effervescent.

On a small throne in the middle of the room sat a woman. She was wearing a red velvet tunic, embroidered with gold vines and flowers. It came up to her neck and folded with her body that sat against the small throne. On her head was a well-worn blond wig that swooped up above her head like a large nest. On top of the wig lay a tasteful and masculine style gold crown. Her left hand was out of my sight, but her right hand rested on her knee, carefully holding a small golden orb. There were indentations on it.

I sat on a stool, our eyes level. I was not nervous anymore. We sat looking at each other for a moment.

"How are you?" she asked me.

"I'm fine, though the journey over was cold." I tentatively replied.

She had a rich Russian accent and the tone of her voice was comically low, like she was purposefully altering her register.

"The time we have tonight should be used wisely, do you understand?" She said.

"Yes, I only have a few questions before we begin. Do you mind if I take notes?" I said, pulling a small notepad from my pocket.

"I don't think you understand." She said.

This woman seemed strangely familiar to me, but I couldn't quite place where she was from.

"What about this do I not understand?" I asked her, I started to take notes, despite her lack of response.

Her eyes drifted from me slowly along the wall, as if trying to find something, behind me. Her eyes looked tired and watery. The air was shifting again.

"That was my father," she said in her low, accented voice, her eyes staring beyond me.

I turned my head to look where she was looking. There was a large black and white photograph of a round-headed man, dressed in a dark suit with a carnation in the lapel. I knew who this man was, somehow. As I turned my head to return my focus, the last glimpse of the photograph, the eyes moved. I was un-startled by it.

She was now standing, and the golden orb had been dropped to the ground. "It's time for us to leave," she said, her voice now returning to a normal pitch, the accent gone. She moved towards the door and gestured to me to follow. As she turned her back to me, I could see that the wig only covered the crown of her head, and she was completely bald in the back. The air didn't feel sparkly anymore.

I followed her through the door, where we met with the short slim man who had led me into the room. The three of us made our way out of the apartment, down the stairs and out the front door onto the street.

We walked quickly along the path and out to the main street, where there was now traffic and people everywhere. No one paid attention to us. As we walked along the street I realized that the front of the tunic with its gold embroidery had lost its shimmer and seemed dull now, and the red fabric looked cheap, purple in the blue street lights. The wig was slipping down the right side of her head as we took hurried strides down the busy street.

We made it to the subway. We walked down the stairs to the turnstiles and I went through first, the woman following me. The turtleneck-clad man was stopped from entering, but we kept walking.

"It's good to get away isn't it!?" She exclaimed suddenly. "Noone knows who I am here," she said in an Australian accent.

I could now see that there were large holes along the sides of her tunic. She was an imposter, her wig was falling off as she made her way to the opposite side of the platform, away from me. She looked at me and waved goodbye, with fresh excitement in her eyes. Trains arrived on our opposite platforms, each going in different directions. She climbed into her carriage and I stepped onto mine. I caught her eye through the windows, just in time for her to wink at me as our trains began to move away from the platform, away from each other.

***

"When I woke up I realized it was my mother, and the photograph was of my grandfather."

My therapist seemed happy with my first reaction to the dream.

"What is your mother to you? We have talked about her before and some of the troubles you had growing up." She seemed relieved to have a clear goal for our session.

"She can be a difficult woman. She has issues acknowledging her poor mental health and used alcohol to cope a lot of the time, which made things difficult for a long time. But now our relationship is mostly good. I worked hard to set specific boundaries with her a few years ago. It takes constant practice to remind her of boundaries."

"Tell me more about the gold orb," she said.

"It was just a gold orb, it was round and gold, like an orb. Around the size of a softball." I fought the urge to smirk.

Why was I being such a smart ass?

"Do any of the things inside the apartment exist in real life? Do you remember any of them?" She asked.

"Not really, even the picture of my grandfather seemed like something I don't remember from real life. The tunic was beautiful at the start, it looked very cool and chic. It was strange and disappointing how everything decayed as she walked"

"Yes, the walk from the second floor of an apartment to the subterrane of the metro is interesting," she was intrigued.

"It was like the more time I spent with her, the faster the air seemed to change. It was unsettling, shifting and moving around from mood to mood... it's hard to explain."

"No, I understand, the mood of the dream seems to start nervous, then turns sparkly, then morphs into something quite sterile and frantic, yes?" She surmised.

"Yeah, something like that. It was strange how quickly things dissolved."

"What did you feel when she dropped the orb?" She was so focused on the orb.

"I didn't feel anything, I don't think. No, I didn't really respond to it."

"Well, it could be a representation of the world that you share with your mother, and that she is dropping it again. You have expressed that she wasn't always present in your childhood" she said.

"She had a difficult life, and I have said many times that having four children was a bit too much for her. At her best, she is a kind, warm and generous woman who can move mountains. At her worst, she is manipulative, juvenile and a bully. She reacts to situations like an actress playing out a well-rehearsed scene and has created a narrative to live by, that only sometimes resembles reality. She changes past events to paint herself as a victim, and I believe she does this to survive. The brain wants to protect itself and the psyche from the worst situations, and if she had to acknowledge the extent of the damage she has caused in her life, that would be a bit too much for her too." I finished.

"When was the last time you spoke to your mother?" she asks.

"About a week ago. I don't exactly rely on her for support. I called her a few months ago when I was crying and she told me to 'shhhhhh' and have a glass of wine and go to bed. That 'shhhhh' was so loud I thought the phone line was busted."

"How did it make you feel when she dismissed you like that?" she asks.

"It's not optimal, but I guess it's the only way she knows how to mother. Again, it's like she's reading it from a script, because it doesn't sound natural. She just wants to say something. It's probably what her mother told her to do when she left my Dad."

"Let's talk about how she led you down into the metro. She took a different train than you - is there a time that she deliberately veered away from you?" She's on a roll now.

"When I was twelve, she was given a choice between her husband who was violent, and me. She chose him. As an adult, I realize this is the behaviour of someone who is in a very controlled and fearful relationship, but as a kid, I just felt rejected. So I moved into my Dad's home. The transition wasn't easy."

The session was almost over, and we'd just hit the intense part. I had talked about the violence in sessions before, but this was the first time it had come up organically as part of a story.

"Look we will have to touch more on this in the next session, I think there is some importance here" she needed to end the call.

***

Keen to move my body, I met Joseph down the street after my session had ended. He was wearing a thick jacket, tights, and running shoes. I smiled and placed a toque on his head.

"Can't run in zero degrees without a hat babe!"

He grins at me.

"How are you doing?" He asks.

"I'm ok, I had a hard session with my therapist. We ran out of time just as we got to the big stuff... I kinda don't want to go for this run."

"We are just doing a few laps of the park though, it will be good!" He's right.

We ran six laps, making a five-kilometre dent in my Fitbit. We were breathless as we headed back to my apartment to warm up.

"I feel so much better after that run," he said. I didn't know he needed it too.

"Me too" I agreed. "Therapy was hard work tonight. My Mum came up because of some weird dream I had."

I could tell Joseph was quietly paying attention. It's not often people open up about things like this. Therapy is usually referenced in a joke or witty comeback. Rarely do people actually share what is said.

We arrived home and sat on the yoga mats I had laid out in the living room. Joseph was new to running and learning he needed to stretch out afterwards. He was not keen on it, but I insisted.

We sat facing each other, our hands clasped together and our legs stretched out, leaning into each other to stretch out our hamstrings.

"She wasn't an easy mother" I carefully offered.

"Why is that?" He wanted to know more. How much more?

"Well, I don't think she should have had more than two kids. I think four were too much for her. She told me when I was young that I was a 'marriage-saving baby' and I didn't know what it meant. I asked my Dad, and he said that if that were true, then why did they divorce when I was two?" Joseph was paying less attention to our stretches now. So I carried on "She left my Dad when I was two years old. He had just gotten out of hospital and six months of rehabilitation from his spinal injury. I never understand who could leave a man who was in a wheelchair, especially so soon after it happened. It seems pretty selfish to me. I'm not sure my Dad or the rest of my family could ever forgive her for that."

"Oh my god." Joseph exhaled out of the stretch.

I had already told Joseph about my father's bicycle accident and resulting paraplegia. He felt nothing below his armpits. He had been in a wheelchair since 1991.

We shifted on the mats to do back stretches side by side.

"One of my earliest memories of her is holding my head to her chest as she yelled down the phone to my Dad. I would have been about four years old. She started dating again too. I was told that she broke up a marriage, then dumped the poor guy a few weeks later. She dated an undertaker who would show up at our house in his hearse and bring us, sweets, then tell us stories about the dead people he took care of at the mortuary. She met someone at a dinner party when I was about six, a bald, imposing guy called Peter. Peter was loud and mean, he had a thick, grey moustache and big eyes that seemed to protrude from their sockets when he was angry, which was pretty often. Even as a kid I was frightened of him. He was so quick to discipline."

Joseph was listening intently as we rolled onto our bellies. Hands under shoulders, we pushed up to stretch out our torsos, and I kept talking. There was no stopping me now.

"I remember they got married very quickly, and it was around then that I started overhearing things, snippets of adults' conversations when they thought the children weren't listening. Things my parents would say, things my aunts and uncles would say. My Mum has five siblings and there are nineteen grandkids, and we were close at that time. Sometimes they'd wait until they thought the kids were out of earshot, other times they weren't so subtle. The tone of our family gatherings, which had always been the most blissfully chaotic events, turned serious. I tried to observe and understand the shift in the adults' moods. They all confirmed what I had quietly suspected: he was a bad guy. They all called him names, and it seemed like everyone knew that he was bad except for my Mum. Someone would try to talk to her about it, which would immediately prompt a loud argument with yelling and swearing before she'd throw us into the car and leave prematurely. My sister and I would wave out the window to our cousins, disappointed we couldn't finish playing, but somehow knowing not to argue. My mum and her new husband were involved in a pyramid selling scam called Amway. They were in over their heads and owed money to a lot of people. They tried to rope in anyone they could, including Mum's friends. They were perfect targets: they had a lot of money and a lot of spare time. Unfortunately for her, they were also smart enough to spot a scheme and so, a lot of them stopped talking to her. Friends she'd known for years, who'd helped her out when Dad was in the hospital and she had four little kids, just couldn't cope with her anymore. When I was nine, we moved two hours down the coast out of Melbourne, away from my Dad."

We moved onto hands and knees, flexing and contracting our backs. I continued with my story, Joseph's poised silence egged me on

"Things were fine for a little while, but I think Mum suffered unbearable regret. She'd moved because Peter wanted to, and she'd left two of her children in Melbourne. She'd split up her kids and kept us from our Dad, all to satisfy Peter, who her whole family disliked. Once she picked me up from school in a terrible mood. Her moods were always a total wild card, and I dreaded these days. It was like waiting for a volcano to explode, spitting off molten hot lava insults, with no regard to the damage she inflicted. She yelled at the teacher supervising the pick-up. I was so embarrassed and knew that this wouldn't be the only insult she'd spit. The week before that I'd had some friends over after school and we were playing in the garden. She had suddenly yelled at us for no apparent reason, and I was absolutely mortified. So when she showed up yelling at the school that day, I'd had enough. I yelled back at her. She looked shocked - maybe she was about to be embarrassed. She grabbed me roughly by the arm and dragged me into the car. Once the doors were closed and no one else could hear, she started screaming at me. I don't even remember what she said, just that I was a little bit proud that I'd stood up to her. I was so tired of walking on eggshells, not knowing what version of Mum I'd get to experience from one day to the next. We lived about a twenty-minute drive from the school, but she quickly tired from yelling at me. She stopped the car and kicked me out, telling me to walk home. So I did, and it took an hour."

Joseph looked at me, visibly concerned. We sat, leaning forward over our legs.

"Less than a year later, we moved house, closer into town. That's when the violence between me and her husband started. My Mum had to start working at the hospital to make ends meet, and my sister, Caroline, had started high school and was gone most of the day. It was just him and I a lot of the time. I started to regurgitate some of the things I'd heard the adults around me say and echoed their words. None of the violence was my fault, I know that now as an adult, but I did say things that provoked him." I continued

"Like what?" Joseph asked.

"That he was a conman, and that he was a loser. My Dad often called him a criminal, so I did one day too. We were in the car when I said this, and he stopped on the side of the road, pulled me out of the car and threw me onto the gravel. Then he picked me up and dragged me back into the car, and we drove home in silence. When we got home he pulled me out of the car again, dragged me up the steps through the front door, then threw me onto my bed where I cowered into a ball. He stood over me, yelling and screaming for a solid five minutes. He did this thing when he was angry, where he pointed his first and pinky fingers at his victim as if he could emphasize his anger through this gesture. I was covered in dirt and scratches, too scared to come out of my room until my Mum came home. She was tired and played everything down. She did every time something like that happened. She ignored all the signs, the bloody noses, the scratches and bruises. I had a broken ankle once from him pushing me down the stairs, and she told the doctor I tripped."

"Oh my god, I am so sorry" Joseph gasped.

"One night when I was twelve it got really bad. My sister Caroline and I were fighting both of them about something. Caroline ran to her room at one point. Peter held me down on the ground and punched me square in the face. I still remember the feeling of my head jolting back like that. My nose wasn't broken, and it stopped bleeding after about ten minutes, but it has never really looked the same. Anyway, we were both sent to our rooms and my Mum and he left to go to a bar, telling us that we were horrible children. When the car had safely pulled away, Caroline called our uncle who lived close by, and he came and picked us up. We took our school bags and a few changes of clothes."

By this stage, Joseph and I were sitting comfortably, relaxing. Our stretching was done. We sat up against the wall, side by side, and he took my hand.

"What happened after that?" he asked softly.
"We lived with our uncle and his wife and kids for a month or so, to finish the school term. Plans were made around me without asking me what I wanted to do. It was weird but I didn't want to leave my Mum there with Peter. She put all of my sister and my things on the porch one day, so my sister and I made the move back to Melbourne. My dad had a three-bedroom house he shared with my step mum Lorraine, and my older sister and brother lived with them too. The house was crowded and I was depressed. When I was thirteen I started to get happy again. I didn't talk to my mother for two and a half years. I was in high school

and had a part-time job. I had just started getting into running and things were looking normal. Then when I was sixteen Peter kicked Mum out of their house, or she left - the whole thing is still a bit unclear. There was a collective sigh of relief in the family, and I don't know, I just went along with everyone else. Mum moved into a small one-bedroom apartment in Melbourne and got a job. I started seeing her again. I was still so mad at her, though I never really let on. I did all the things you are supposed to do, went for dinner, visited, consoled her when her mum died, even when Peter showed up at the funeral and she sat with him instead of her children. She obviously started dating again within a year. She was going through a series of men whose wives had died, and she'd known them, even been friendly with them. It was kind of terrible," I concluded.

I felt like I had been talking for too long.

"Anyway, you probably don't want to hear this," I said.
"No, I do, I mean as much as you want to share. It's very interesting," Joseph replied.

I stood up to make tea. As I switched the kettle on, Joseph came up behind me and held me in a long hug. He liked to do this. We are the same height, and it is comforting. He is sweet.

"I didn't mean to tell all this, a lot of it is in the past. I keep my Mum at arm's length now for these reasons. I don't really know if I can trust her." I wondered if I'd shared too much.

We carried our tea back to the yoga mats. I wanted to finish the story to let Joseph know I had put all of that behind me.

"I kept her at arm's length for years. She would call me or I would call her once a month or so. She would deposit some money into my Australian bank account every birthday. I've lived in Canada for ten years now and she's been to visit me once," I said.

"Only once?" Joseph seemed surprised.

We sip our tea, and I pause for a minute. Looking into his eyes is relaxing.

"She is a difficult woman. She knows she has made mistakes, and she continues to make them. She is frantic and wild, or dead asleep. There is no in-between. She is the life of every party but also very impatient. She does this strange thing with her voice where she tries to sound raspy, sick and run down. I think she thinks it will garner some sympathy from everyone around her. She is complex." I took a sip of my tea

"Sounds like it," Joseph said.

"Her upbringing was strange. She grew up surrounded by wealth, with butlers and nannies and drivers and gardeners and housekeepers and a summer house. Her dad, my grandfather, was a very successful businessman. All the stories I've heard about him make him sound like an asshole, to be honest. He had a whole other family that she didn't know about until she was in her 20's. I imagine that is why she seems to have trust issues with men, yet she depends on them. I don't think she will ever be single." I stated.

"Do you know anything about the other family?" Joseph asked.

"Nope. Someone pointed out a lady that is supposedly my half-aunt to me once at a funeral, that's about it," I said, dismissively.

I was starting to realize that one day, Joseph might meet my Mum. Is it unfair to give him this much information? I try to balance it out.

"I don't say any of this to make her out to be a villain, it's just that there is such nuance to our relationship. My oldest sister Anne is her favourite, she will do anything for her and her kids. And that works fine for her, as she barely talks to my brother Victor, or sees his kids."

I had been talking for an hour now. It was nine pm, approaching Joseph's bedtime. We said good night at my door, and I hugged him a little tighter than normal. He kissed me and smiled. "Thanks for sharing", he said softly. He pulled his face mask up and walked into the hallway, pressed the button for the elevator and turned back to face me.

"So I'll see you on Thursday night?" He called out.
"Yes, Thursday night."
"Love you" I could see his smile under his mask.
"Love you too."

He disappeared into the elevator.

I slumped back into my apartment.
My shoulders and chest felt loose and relaxed after all that talking.

CHAPTER 5

I have a strange intuition within me. The weekend before the Covid lockdowns, I purchased a new comforter set. An air mattress I eyed on my way to the counter was heavily discounted, so it made sense to buy it. There had been reports from China about the Coronavirus, but it seemed a whole world away. I had strangely done a lot of travel in the five weeks before the covid lockdowns. It was like I was trying to put a year's worth of travel and seeing people important to me.

Most governments had hinted towards a lockdown, but none had confirmed it. People were still anxious though, and the day they emptied the shelves of toilet paper and dried pasta, my sister called me. Caroline was in New York from Australia for a conference, and asked if she could come and stay with me in Toronto for a few weeks while this 'lockdown' period was happening. We thought, along with everybody else, we'd stay home for 14 days and flatten the curve, then carry on with our lives.

Caroline slept on that air mattress, under the comforter set I had bought on a whim, for four months during the first wave, when it was impossible to get a flight back to Australia.

THE DETERMINIST

At times it was difficult being two grown siblings living in a one bedroom apartment with 'stay at home' pleas from the government. But with enough imagination and wine, we made it work. We even began to enjoy it. It's not often you get a chance to spend that much time with someone who has been your best friend since you were an infant.

Now the impromptu comforter is on my bed. I am laying on my bed in the middle of the day on a Tuesday because there is nothing better to do than read a book.

I look down at the comforter pattern. With its pink lacy pattern winding in and out of purple spots, it is new age-developed kitsch. Just like my tapestry of flowers and bees, in the right light... it almost looks tasteful.

Before lockdown, this was a true luxury, lying in the autumn sun, on a bed, reading a book, basking in the warmth and serenity of it all. Now it's regular. However, it is a nice break for my mind, as the global catastrophe of the pandemic leans away from me at this moment.

My phone buzzes. It's Anthony texting me, pulling me out of my daydream.

'Alright gay boy, any subjects off limits tonight?' the text says.

Anthony was coming with his girlfriend Francesca to my apartment for dinner, mainly to meet Joseph. I was nervous about this. Anthony, albeit a genuinely kind and warm friend, had become aggressive and sometimes downright mean over the pandemic. During the first lockdown, Caroline couldn't tolerate him.

'Why, are you planning on being rude?' I replied.

'Well so far I have extrapolated;
Scared of Francesca, a five ft, beautiful twenty-two year old,
Cannot tolerate crowds of 4 or more,
Bedtime is nine pm,
Paint me a better picture, because I am genuinely scared I might make this guy cry... do I have to be proper?'

His incomplete sentences punched me quickly, one after the other.

I had made a huge error in trying to play it cool with Anthony about this. I should have just told him that I needed his help impressing this guy.

'You have no duty other than to help your nervous friend navigate this portion of dating in his 30's. So just be your charming self and remember that I like this guy, that's all that needs to really matter.' I replied, almost panting from texting so fast. Suddenly my serene reading bed was a hot and uncomfortable mass underneath me.

'Are *YOU* nervous? We should have done this on Friday so I can have a few drinks, really throw the cat amongst the pigeons' He pinged back.

'Of course I am nervous...' I replied, hoping for mercy.

'Well now I am excited. What are you cooking now that Big Joe is here?' Anthony could always be relied upon to talk food.

'I'm trying to figure that out now, sirloin tip roast, it takes 3 hours and has the chance of being tough. Or I'll just make chicken and keep it simple. I mean I don't even eat meat, but...' I read the text back to myself after I had sent it. Sirloin tip roast?

'Buy strip loins and I'll bring my cast iron and Joe will be blown away... BLOWN AWAY.

I can buy the strip loins on my way over if you need.' Was he being supportive or condescending?

I am not happy about Anthony nicknaming Joseph without even meeting him. It's a posture of ego, to assert some kind of familial dominance over someone he hasn't met. An argument for another time.

'This is perfect, I'll go to the market now to buy the strip loins... Thanks, buddy, I appreciate this.' Maybe we were back to normal.

Sometimes, showing vulnerability to such a controlling man is the only way to gain any leverage as a gay man. It's a true paradigm shift. It's like the straight best friend is just looking for a reason to help without feeling used. It's a cousin of misogyny that needs its own name.

I collect myself and roll off the bed, walk to the front door and dress for the outside.

It is an easy fall day as the sun is setting behind the condos of downtown Toronto. I feel more confident now that there is a plan in place. Making my way towards the market, the breeze is cool against my face. I am dressed nicely, my hair is falling just the way I want, and I have friends coming over soon to meet my new boyfriend.

I pull my mask up over my mouth and nose across the street from the market. I walk straight in, there is no lineup this time of day. As I walk into the building, a set of eyes hit mine from across the market vestibule.

It is Arthur White, a friend of my ex-boyfriend, Robert. I used to get along well with him. He is a haughty man, standing at around 6 foot 6 and morbidly obese. He has a melancholic face and swollen eyes. I don't think I have ever seen him smile. Keeping pace walking into the store, I hope that he won't notice me.

Breathing through the first pang of panic, my shoulders return to their normal lower stance.

Given the pandemic, there seems to be an unwritten flow to the store in the produce section. I feel like a reconnaissance spy in a movie, keeping an eye out for the mark, while vigilantly keeping count of the vegetables I'm selecting, making sure I don't have to break a new pandemic social law, and double back.

Approaching the butcher counter, I contemplate the striploin. Ordering the cuts takes a few moments, and as I collect my package off the counter, I have the feeling that someone is looking at me. I turn, looking for him again.

"Hello young man." Arthur's lyrical way of talking is soft, yet audible over the hubbub of the market.

"Arthur! As I live and breathe... how are you?" I feel relieved. What was I expecting?

"How have you been?" Arthur cocks his head to the side.
"I'm great! Things are bubbling along well given the current climate, how about you?" I replied quickly, my cadence is always faster when startled.

"Oh well, it's difficult, I see my clients online, it's been difficult, I haven't seen Robert in a few months, this time has been hard on him," Arthur said, his eyes wandering around my face looking for subtle hints of emotional reaction on saying my ex's name.

"Yeah, I was keeping up with him, but lost touch over the last few months. I think it has been a hard time for him." I said, wishing the ground would swallow me whole.

"How are things financially?" Arthur asked.

My only determination from him asking me this is that he is in an even worse financial situation than he was before the pandemic.

"Oh you know me, I will always be financially good. I am smart with money. I worked the first five months of the pandemic at 80 hours a week, I am taking some time off"

He glances at my shopping basket.

Shallots, garlic, organic herbs and $45 worth of prime beef steak. I feel bashful.

"I have been meaning to reach out, I have been so busy over the last few months, catching up for a drink or a coffee at some stage would be nice. I miss seeing you." A blend of subtle lies and sharp truths fell out of my mouth.

"Looks like you're having a party of sorts?" Arthur said, still fixed on my basket.

"Oh, yeah, you remember Anthony? Well, he and his girlfriend are coming for dinner to meet my boyfriend, so I thought I would make something nice." Why do I offer up this much information?

"Look I better get on, it was great seeing you Arthur, I would really like to catch up soon."

"Just send me an email, I would like to catch up too," he answered looking dejected.

Hug, handshake, shoulder bump... I just moved away cautiously and passed him saying goodbye. He reaches out and touches my hair. I pretend not to notice. I just turn and keep walking.

I call Anthony on my way home from the store.
"You are never going to guess what just happened to me. Not only do we have delicious steaks for tonight that will be cooked to perfection, but I just had one of the most awkward interactions of my life with one of your best friends." I said, seething sarcasm.

Anthony pauses for a moment before answering.

"Who? Did you get the steaks?" he asked.

"I bumped into Arthur White," I declared, hoping for a laugh.
"No, that pedophile fuck? I thought he would be dead by now." Not quite the response I was anticipating.

Anthony has a way of being wrong, so wrong that he defames not only the person he is talking about but so wrong that it makes me worry for Anthony himself, simply for saying something so outrageous.

"Firstly he is not a pedophile, you idiot. Not all aged gays are pedophiles. Secondly... He reached out and touched my hair. It was the weirdest thing." I instantly regret telling him this.

"Seriously, he reached out and just touched your hair... and you don't think this man is a pedophile?" Anthony said sharply.

"He is gross, but not that, Anthony"

"But he just reached out and touched your hair, invading your personal space, like a pedophile."

"Anthony, I am 30. He is not a pedophile"

"Whatever man. We will be there for six pm" Anthony said, drawing the conversation to a close.

***

It is so uncomfortable talking to a therapist about weird sex dreams.

"So you had this dream the night after the dinner party?"

"Yes, also, I should probably mention I ran into Arthur White that day too, and it was uncomfortable," I added, having just jumped the hurdle of telling my therapist about the strange dream.

Arthur and my therapist had been colleagues. Arthur's referral was how I started going to therapy in the first place.

"Mhmm, so just go over the main part of this dream again." she led.

I hadn't written and emailed it to her like I normally do, as this one was a bit disgusting, and I had been putting it off for a few days. So I decided to recite it for her in the session. She scribbled fiercely as I talked. I would pay double the fee for this session if I could read her notes afterwards.

"So, I was in a park, and Robert and two other guys were sitting on a bench. We all went back to a house, everyone but me stripped down naked. A drugged-up skinny guy was on the bed and Robert started having very fast and rough sex with him on the bed while I was watching, and the other two guys were just standing there." I started.

"Do you recognize the skinny man on the bed?" she queried.
"No, but after a while, things were getting rougher. Then one of the other guys in the room moved towards me and started pulling my head down by my hair and punched me in the face. It wasn't like he was going to do anything sexual, but he wanted to hurt me. I ran away from them and went to a room off to the side, and called out for Robert." I was getting more graphic now.

"Do you know where this room was?" She asked.
"It looked a little like the room in an apartment I had a few years ago... so I came out of the side room and went back into the bedroom and it was just Robert. He was crying and we talked for a while. He told me that they had killed the skinny guy after they had finished. It was messed up. I remember being scared in the dream." I was still a bit scared.

"Could you see any of the other people in the room anymore?"
"No," I replied. It was a lie. I knew those men. They were friends of Roberts who were difficult to talk about. The main person was Ronnie. Ronnie was terrible to me over the years.

"What did you do on the day of the dream?" she kept going.

" I had Anthony and his girlfriend over to meet Joseph. It was a really great night. It was that afternoon that I ran into Arthur White in the supermarket. He looked terrible, I think the lockdowns have been hard on him." I clarified the order of events.

"I know that he and Robert were close friends, how was the interaction with Arthur?" she asked.

"It was fine, I am glad that I was wearing nice clothes and looked good... he just, he kinda reached out and touched my hair though, that was weird," I confessed.

"He touched your hair?" she looked up from her notepad.

"Yeah, he like, grabbed a lock of my hair and twirled my curls in his fingers. It was fast but so strange. I know that Arthur is a colleague of yours, we can talk about something else if you need to." I gave her the out.

"You don't need to worry about Arthur. What we say in here is confidential," she assured me.

"Ok, well, it reminded me of something that I hadn't thought about in years. It's a bit gross." I continued.

"Mhmm, what happened?" She moved in closer to the camera, still scribing onto a notepad.

"Well, it reminded me of a small gathering I went to a few years ago at Arthur's. There were a few people there, all from the gay hockey team, just middle-aged gay guys. And one of them started asking Robert questions about me, while I was sitting right next to them." I wasn't about to tell her that the person asking the questions was Arthur.

"What kind of questions?" She asked.

"Asking about my... sexual performance. Look, I'll spare you the details but this group of men had a lengthy discussion about my ability to perform certain sex acts, while I was sitting next to them. They were all leering at me while talking. It was gross." I started to feel anxious telling her this.

I could see my therapist getting more and more intrigued and worried about this conversation

"Was Robert ok with this? Was Arthur?" she asked.

I weighed up the next words in my head. Arthur was her colleague, but this was my therapy.

"The bulk of the conversation was egged on by Arthur, and Robert was very enthusiastically telling them stories about our sex life," I replied.

"Did you say anything to Robert to try and make him stop?" She sounded bewildered as I described this type of conversation.

"No. I just sat there. I think at the time I sort of liked the attention. I was 24. I was still running a lot so I was very lythe. And this was a room of middle-aged hockey players all over 6 feet, and... Arthur, It was a little intimidating." This felt more like a confession.

"Did you talk to Robert about this afterwards?" she asked again.

"I don't remember," I said to her.

"In the dream, Robert seems to be regretful. Is this something that he used to display after things like this?" she moved the subject back to the dream with a click of her pen.

"I remember in the last three years of our relationship when things had become really bad, he would say terrible things to me, and then would cry and say sorry, then we would cry together, then go for a walk. In the early days, we'd have sex. It was a horrible cycle. Usually, I was trying to call him out on things that he had said." I replied uncomfortably.

"Like what?" She asked.

"Like when he used to call me fat. I wasn't overweight. It's just that there is so much pressure in the gay community to look a certain way. And he definitely made me feel that pressure. It was so demeaning." The words fell out of me now.

"Was that the only thing you used to fight about?" she pressed.

"No, he was quite frequently rude to my friends, and I used to apologize for him a lot. He was this loud and dumb character who I used to find endearing, and now I cannot stand it." I hadn't articulated this to myself yet. There is already so much unpack in this session. I decide not to talk about infidelity. But I can feel myself getting bothered.

"When he was rude to your friends, how did you react?" She asked.

"He had a way of saying things that were ultimately aimed at me, most of the time. Once, he was complimenting Anthony's abs, but then said 'why can't Greg have abs like that?' It was so uncomfortable." I tried to explain the nuances of his berating comments.

"How did that make you feel when he did that?" She asked.

"Horrible. Worthless, like I was wasting his time by being with him." The words fell out of me again.

Our session was drawing to a close.

"When you think about the way you used to feel, do you feel better now that he is not in your life?" She asked, leading the answer.

"Yeah, I guess, but I feel kind of guilty for talking to myself that way. And being made to feel like that." It's complex, this guilt.

***

When the session ended, I sat alone in my apartment, poured myself a glass of wine, and began to feel anxious.

How did I let myself down like that? It is hard to imagine enduring that level of self-loathing for so long. Having it egged on by an external force for so long. Egged on by the person you were supposed to be able to trust above everyone else.

Looking around my living room, my eyes fall to a small picture frame in the corner, which contains a photograph of Robert and I with his niece and nephew. We are all giving a thumbs up to the camera. Walking over to it, I stub my toe on the coffee table, pick up the frame and look at the four smiling faces, taken two Christmases ago. My toe is bleeding from where I stubbed it on the furniture. I walk through the kitchen to get a bandaid and instinctively throw the picture in its frame into the trash can, pausing to watch some old food spill onto it.

Sitting against my bathtub, applying a bandage to my toe I begin to cry. I slowly walk to the kitchen, open the freezer to get an ice pack and open the trash to retrieve the picture. Washing off the frame, I spend a moment looking at it. We were all so smiley then. Setting the frame down off the coffee table, I place the icepack on my toe and retrieve my glass of wine. I have a small cry for the life I once had, back when we were smiley, back when I thought he loved me.

CHAPTER 6

The lightness of Stuart's laugh and the ease of his smile is instantly disarming. When we first met, he was training me in a restaurant in downtown Toronto. I was 22, small in frame, still a timid person trying to figure out how to mesh all the parts of myself together. He was a bright, comfortable figure with an unflappable sense of confidence.

He was tall, broad-shouldered and handsome. He had a deep voice that called everyone "divine", "hunty" and "sugar" with an east coast twang. He made a real show of this confidence, and only performed for himself, there was no regard for anyone else in his vicinity. He had mastered what a lot of young gay men tried to emulate, the perfect balance of masculinity and camp.

Extolling friendship advice was his main virtue, and colleagues in the restaurant relied on him for comfort and advice on problems like lipstick colour and where to take a new boyfriend for dinner.

On our second training shift together, he hugged me. I winced...

"What was that? Are you not a hugger?" he asked, with an almost confrontational tone.

"No, I am just very sunburnt after the beach yesterday," I replied.

"Oh you little pale boy, got your naked arse burnt to a crisp," he said in sympathy.

After eight years he hasn't stopped addressing me by the nickname 'suncrisp'. Some of his friends are not aware of my actual name.

During the first weeks of the lockdown, he was pedantic about the risk. All his food was delivered, and at one point, when he thought he had the virus, he called me to his building where he threw his keys down from his second-floor apartment so I could clear out the contents of his mailbox. I never asked him how he removed garbage from his dwelling.

As the pandemic went on, he was judgmental of my continuing to work, and my frequent visits to Anthony's apartment for dinner.

We would meet for video chats every few days, to talk about guys we had matched with on Tinder, Hinge and Grindr. His persistence in dating was admirable, always looking for love.

It is hard to feel fraternal in gay society. I think we both cherished the ease in how our friendship worked. To have a person who lifts you up, who you can look up to and ask for help is rare.

When I first realized that I needed to end my relationship with Robert, the self-doubt I felt on every level was consuming. I had a daily ritual of asking myself 'what am I even worth?' It became a perpetual chant in my mind. Stuart came over for coffee one day, and after months of keeping this all to myself, he pierced me open with one sentence.

"Suncrisp, darling, I want you to know you look like shit right now." He lovingly observed.

He was right, I had stopped taking care of myself.

Sitting on the mezzanine of Robert's and my home, I knew he was right. Cutting my own hair had become the norm for me over those years, in an effort to impress Robert with my thriftiness. He criticized and commented on my body weight so frequently that I felt like my physique disgusted him, and thus, our relationship problems were blamed on my appearance. His inability to be attracted by anything other than a skinny frame was somehow my failure, so I started starving myself. It was spring, my skin was sallow and pale. I reeked of anxiety and low self-esteem.

I remember the hot feeling in my eyes. That shift of my shoulders and neck muscles.
I told Stuart I was starting to hate myself. He didn't look away from me. He sat watching me cry while I tried to explain the reasons why I hated myself so much. He never shifted in his chair, and when I calmed down, he cleared his throat.
"Tell me 30 reasons why you love yourself," he said softly.

It was like being punched in the face.

I stammered out a few words about running, about travel.

"You know there are more reasons than that darling," he said with a wink.

THE DETERMINIST

***

Stuart and I sat on the stoop of a closed drag bar on Church street drinking coffee in the afternoon sun. We hadn't spent much time together over the last few weeks, the summer of the pandemic saw him go on socially distanced dates, staying six feet apart, wearing masks and constantly sanitizing his hands.

"Suncrisp, I am going to need to see a picture of this boy you have been talking about," he said.

I pulled out my phone and showed him Joseph's Instagram profile.

"He is divine, devoooonity!" he cooed, chin pointed to the sky.

"Show me his dating profile," he continued.
"I can't, I deleted all my dating stuff," I said, sighing.

His eyes looked out onto the street, then dramatically glanced at his coffee.

"All of them? Grindr, Scruff, Tinder?" His brow was furrowed.
I started laughing and he continued.
"Hinge, Bumble, Squirt, Hornet, Guy Spy...?" This was getting comical.

"I guess, yeah."

"Oh, so you are serious about this guy!" He seemed excited.

"Well, no I just... I know it sounds corny, but I wasn't looking for someone in particular, but it's him, he just was there. Perfectly." I replied, sipping my coffee.

"Oh my good lord, hunty... what's he like?" I could see this exchange playing out like a crafted romantic comedy scene in Stuart's mind.

"He is smart, he is beautiful, so beautiful. He has a Ph.D." I started.

"What's his Ph.D. in?" Stuart asked, looking taken aback.

"Fuck, he told me, but I can't remember. I want to remember, but I can't... It's something science-related, in biological chemistry, and he has told me twice already." I admitted, hating that I couldn't remember.

"Oh honey," his eyes roll into the back of his head.

We both sip our coffees and look out onto the street. It's hard looking out onto the bars we used to frequent. Before all of this started, the pandemic, once a week he and I would be at a drag show, or an event. Stuart is on a gay social planning committee and organizes drag shows and trivia nights. He is an extrovert's extrovert.

There is sadness sitting on the corner. Nothing to do but drink coffee on a Friday afternoon. I feel Stuart shift in his seat and pull himself up.

"Well, how's the sex?" No topic is off-limits.
"Interesting that you ask"

I am dreading this question from him. I knew I needed to open up to him about this.

"He is incredibly understanding of something. This is a little hard to talk about." I prepared.

I feel the weight of what I am about to launch into telling him. I have been carrying this secret around for months. I know how protective Stuart is over me. This is a topic I was hoping to address later on, after the pandemic.

"There are certain things in bed that I cannot do." I started.

"Why is everything alright?" he sharply looked at me before taking a small sip of his coffee.

"Do you remember how I was in Miami in February, to run that marathon? It was a few weeks before the lockdown." I need to trail off my conversation to give him some time to brace for what I planned to say.

He nodded, "yeah, what happened?"

"The night before the race, I had a guy over to my hotel room. He was very good-looking, very Miami, tan, muscled… so, he and I spent an hour together and it was great, really good sex. Then he messaged me the next day after I had run the marathon. I told him I needed time because, well I had just run a marathon… I told him I needed to eat, he said he would come and get me and take me out to a place he knew." I could feel Stuart's eyes on me. I looked straight forward. "When I messaged him to come over he was there within five minutes, and he was… aggressive."

"Jesus, how aggressive?" Stuart asked.

"Well, he walked into my hotel room, and pushed me towards the bed and turned me around. I started saying 'stop' and tried to push him away from me." I continued.

"Oh fuck, Suncrisp" Stuart's face dropped.

I continued, I needed this story out of me.

" ...and then he just kinda went for it, and I just lay there trying to figure out what to do. He had his hand around my throat and was just pushing himself further and further into me and whispering into my ear that I wanted it. It was probably a minute or two, but I finally managed to push him off me. I got my foot in the crease of his hip and kicked him backwards. He went backwards weirdly, colliding with the TV stand, which grazed the side of his head." I stopped, taking a sip from my coffee.

"What the fuck?" Stuart's reaction made me acknowledge how bad it was.

"He looked a little shocked and said something about hurting his head, but I think he could see that I was bleeding. I was on the other side of the room at this point while he got himself together and he started calling me names while I repeatedly told him to leave." I finished.

"Did you call the police?" Stuart asked.

"I was in Florida, what was I supposed to say to them? I'd had a beer with some other runners on the way home from the race, and it wasn't like he didn't have scratches on him too. I honestly was so exhausted and in shock" I finished.

"What the fuck? What did you do? Wait, you went on to New York after that right?" He wanted every detail now.

"Yeah, so I left Miami the next morning. Picked up some tampons and had to wear them for a few days. I just went to New York and spent time with my sister and some friends. I didn't talk to anyone about it. Not even my therapist... I didn't even go to the doctor about it, I didn't think it was that bad, but I have a fissure, and it is ok sometimes and bad sometimes.." I trailed off.

"Jesus, Suncrisp. I am so sorry. What did you say to Joseph?" He understood what I meant about my bedroom limitations now.
"I talked to him about it very unemotionally. Just gave him the facts. He was very understanding and kind. He told me I had to go to the doctor. So I went last week, I told the doctor everything. He examined me and prescribed an ointment."

"Did you talk to someone about this? Christ Suncrisp, you were raped" He wanted me to hear the weight of this the way he had.

I hadn't used that word for what had happened to me yet. I hadn't heard it being used by anyone I had talked to about it. Rape is a big word that carries big implications and labels that I wasn't ready for. I don't like feeling like a victim.

We kept drinking our coffee.

The sun started to come through the clouds. The street became quiet for a moment. There was a rare moment of silence between Stuart and me.

"Please promise me you will not put yourself in these situations again Suncrisp. After all those men in the bad times, when you started living alone, I was genuinely worried. And I'm still surprised that nothing like this happened to you in those times. Just, well, fuck, it's not right." Stuart said, looking exacerbated.

I tried not to take judgement from his words. I leaned in and put my arm on his arm.

"I'm ok now, I know.." my sentence trailed off, I had nothing left to say.

We say our goodbyes. Watching Stuart walk away from me I notice that he is stepping a little softer. His head is down and his gait is longer.

Walking down the street I start to shake the feeling of the conversation. I step on my heels to make a louder sound. My hips are swaying and I am feeling better. A grin arrives under my mask, there is no one around, so I take the mask off and breathe in the fall air. I feel lighter.

At home, I sit for a minute looking out my window. The sun is setting.
Preparing for a run, lacing my shoes up and covering my face and head, I decide to leave earphones at home, normally a running essential.

Making my way out of the building, down the now busy street, traversing Cabbagetown towards Riverdale, I am running at full speed. It is cold enough that my lungs are hurting and my eyes are watering.

Arriving at the top of the hill at Riverdale Park, my legs are on fire, my lungs are tingling and my hands are numb. I stop, looking west over the city. The sun is entering twilight.

Sitting on the bench looking out over the city, I put my head in my hands. Tears start to form in my eyes. With the sting of hot tears falling down cold cheeks, I start to shudder. And gulp. Breath seems unattainable. The seat feels inviting. I lean back and lay across the length of the bench. Sniffing and shuddering, I hold myself by the knees and keep crying. I have lost the ability to care what onlookers might think. There is now a small moan coming from me as I eke out the last of the tears.

Sitting upright I see little purple dots in the corner of my eyes. Rearranging my face mask and standing up, I move towards the back of the bench to stretch out my legs.

I stumble on the first steps, but then, as I have done many times, I raise my chin, put one foot in front of the other, and make my way back down the hill, towards home.

PART 2

CHAPTER 7

Robert stopped and looked onto the arrivals lounge of Dublin airport. He was oblivious that he was blocking the walkway for the other passengers.

"We are here buddy" he said, looking down at me.

He had slept slumped against me on the cramped red eye flight from Toronto to Dublin. I was tired, and my back hurt from having his large body pressed against me for the seven7 hour flight. I was hungry. I was irritable.

We made our way out of the airport and onto the arrivals area, towards the bus bay.

"How do you always know where to go?" Robert was trying to keep up with me as I moved quickly towards the ticket turnstile.

"Two for Dublin, O'Connell street, please." I requested to the ticketing agent.

THE DETERMINIST

It was late April, springtime in Ireland and we had found cheap plane tickets to Dublin for 10 days. It had been a long winter in Canada. Robert and I had had a difficult few months. Fighting before Christmas, we almost ended our relationship. We'd rekindled and said our sorrys over the new year, and then while snowboarding in January, I fell off the side of a mountain, breaking my arm in three places, leaving it in a cast for three months. The healing process was very painful, there were two broken bones in my hand, one in my wrist, and my shoulder had been dislocated, so my neck was stuck in one position for weeks. Two days after I got the cast off, we booked the flights and planned the trip to Ireland. Robert had convinced me that I could do my physio exercises in the car while we were driving around the countryside.

The bus moved quickly down the M1 to the M50 and dropped us off on O'Connell street. I set out and walked in the direction of the river Liffey. I knew where I was going. Rarely lost in new cities, I find keeping a map in my head easy. Navigation is an infallible strength of mine, and Robert just follows along.

After agreeing that we need to stretch our legs from the flight, we make the journey by foot along the south shore of the river bank towards our hotel. It is too early to check-in, so we leave our bags at the hotel and head out to find breakfast. It is 10 am, the bars are beginning to open. After 10 minutes of walking, we step into a quaint and lovely bar room for something to eat. Robert begins his usual questions to the barmaid.

"I'm a big guy, I need a big breakfast, what should I eat?" he queries with tired yet hopeful eyes.

I smirk as the barmaid points to the menu board and says in a soft voice.

"Something from there."

Robert orders himself breakfast and a cup of tea. I order a Guinness. It is Ireland and I haven't slept yet, so why not?

"Oh yeah, I want Guinness too," he adds.

After three minutes Robert turns to me, "I guess she had something better to do" looking at the half-poured pints sitting on the drip tray with annoyance.

"We are in Ireland Rob, they have to let the beer settle. It's standard... It's culture," I said lowly to him.
"It's stupid." he retorts.

After finishing our breakfast of toast, eggs and stout, we make our way back across the river towards the hotel. My eyes are tired and I wish for a nap, there is too much city to explore... Finally, in the hotel room, I run the shower and step in. Robert follows me into the shower, following a ritual we kept from a more romantic time. We lay down to sleep.

Walking up to the tour desk always makes me feel like a naive simpleton. As a young backpacker, I was always too cool to do such a thing. With Robert, it was always the first stop, despite my ability to plan. Robert approaches the tour desk. A humble-looking middle-aged blond woman is smiling at us. Robert slumps his large body on the counter.

"What's, like, the best thing in Dublin to do? We are here for just two days before we go to Cork," he asks, his fingers pointing at the humble desk clerk. His clumsy attempt at humour is embarrassing, and I hang back, hoping he hadn't offended her.

"Hello," she replies. "What are some of your interests while you are here? There are some lovely churches in the city and you cannot leave without a tour of the Guinness Brewery. Might I suggest-"

"Oh yeah the Guinness factory, we already had Guinness today, that was good" he interrupts her.

Robert's ability to talk over people, especially women, is outstanding. The kind-eyed tourism associate moved behind her desk and fetched some brochures and maps. When she returned, she started unfolding some things and marking them with a pen. She locked eyes with me. I smiled at her.

"A good way to see the city is to divide it into two: the north and south of the river Liffey. On the north side, you have some nice pubs and churches, the Jameson Distillery, and in the south, you have Temple bar, Trinity College and the Guinness brewery tour. Would you like me to put these on a map for you?" she asks, not dropping her eye contact with me.

"That would be lovely, thank you" I replied.
"Is there a city tour bus?" Robert cut in. I cringed.

"Yes, there is the city loop tour that leaves from just outside this office every half hour. You can buy tickets directly from the tour operator," she said, gesturing towards the street where the busses were starting to line up.

Thanking the lady, I collected all the maps. Outside we locate the tour bus and step onboard after talking to the guide. The bus winds us through the city as the guide gives annotations about buildings from the front of the bus.

As the patronage of the bus starts to clear out, Robert puts his hand on my knee, this is the closest form of affection I can expect from him. I am grateful and smile at him. It was little moments like this that give me hope that there will be a return to normalcy. A return to romance.

Our night drifts on. With more stout consumed, we make our way towards the hotel, but there is one more bar I want to go to. It is rumoured to be the oldest bar in Ireland. Making our way into the multi-room bar, I bask in the ambience of the room, there is a fire pit outside wafting the smell of campfire in, a small group of old men playing fiddles in one corner, and the bartender greets us with a nod of his head as we sit down.

"Two pints of Guinness and a whisky please" I request to the kindly bartender.

After a few pints of stout, and listening to the band, we leave the bar and make the short trip back towards the hotel. Robert is excited. He is telling me that the Brazen Head is, now, the best bar he has ever been to. 'Just wow' and 'such ambience' is said a few times.

On the corner of the street, standing in the glow of the streetlights, Robert stops, pulls me in, and kisses me. It was a long kiss.

I was suddenly flooded with hope for romance like I had been out parched in a desert for miles and he was giving me a sip of water.

My mind starts racing, I think: 'this is the turning point,' and convince myself that all of the issues we have had over the last year are beginning to melt away. Maybe he does love me after all this, maybe this is it. A pathway to becoming a happy couple again.

***

From Dublin, we rent a car and drive to Cork for a night, around the Ring of Kerry, and into Limerick. We had spent three days driving around beautiful scenery together, saying nice things to each other. We even fell asleep holding each other in Limerick, our bodies returning to the comfort of each other after a year or so of coldness.

We twisted and turned our way through the countryside heading north. My friend Anthony was from Belfast and had arranged for us to spend a night at his uncle's remote beach-side mansion in County Donegal.

When we arrived, Anthony's uncle, Paul, was warm, funny and a little drunk already. His young wife Trish was a new-age yoga instructor and they had a young toddler together, both had children from previous marriages. The night was filled with bottles of wine and chats about the world, and we were all enjoying ourselves until Robert and Trish started talking more intensely about topics that naturally repelled me.

"These 5G towers they are trying to put up all over Ireland, they are a serious threat, they are going to give us horrible health outcomes, and the government just lets the companies put them up!" piped Trish, in her deep yet sharp Irish accent. As she did, Paul gazed at me with a sigh. I looked at Robert who seemed to be hanging onto every word.

Robert was gullible to the dramatic source of many conspiracies. Back home he had a safe full of silver bullion, because of an impending economic crash he had been convinced of. He had stockpiles of dried beans and bottles of expensive vitamins because a 'massive food shortage' was on his paranoid horizon. Robert was prepared for 'something big.' I had started monitoring his youtube consumption to watch out for conspiracy theorist videos. When I would ask him about why he was doing it, he would tell me I didn't understand, and that I was just coasting along, oblivious to the impending devastation of the world. His eyes would turn big, his expression was serious, yet he couldn't articulate his beliefs in any kind of sophisticated language. It would end in a fight, so I'd pretend to be sweetly naive and convince myself he wasn't harming anyone by being so gullible. It was my least favourite trait of his, and I dreaded any mention of these topics in social situations. I didn't want anyone thinking I agreed with him.

"It's even worse than all the vaccines that they try to make us take. It's absolutely ridiculous" continued Trish.

"Directly across the sea is Scotland, right?" I said to Paul, trying to give us both a break from the conversation.

***

Leaving Donegal and heading to the Giant's Causeway, I could tell something was on Robert's mind. His brow had dropped and he was quiet, which normally meant he was hatching an idea that would have strange outcomes.

THE DETERMINIST

We arrived at the Giant's Causeway, slightly hungover from the night before, and in need of some fresh air and exercise. Robert was still quiet, contemplative.

"You know those 5G towers aren't that big a threat, right?" I said to him.

I could feel the air shift between us.

We keep walking along the foot track of the Causeway.

"And vaccines are just basic science, it is a fact…" I continued.

I knew how he felt about these things. I had pathologized it to no end. My assumption was that he wanted to believe he had some sort of secret, some little nugget of information that made him smarter than the rest of the population. That put him in a 'prepared' category of people who knew a greater risk to people than we knew from ourselves. It was an ego trip. It was a comfort. Somewhere he could rest his head as an outsider.

"Well, time will tell…" he loudly retorted. Looking out onto the ocean, a frustrated look in on his face.

We stopped in a small fishing village on our way into Belfast.

As it was now our standard, we ordered stout and bread.

All of a sudden I was struggling to think of things to say to him. I wanted him to know that I want to keep having the fun and nice time we had been having up until that conversation. I didn't want him to feel bad. It was a minor thing that so far hadn't had much effect on our lives. But I could tell he felt like I was looking down on him.

"Are you excited for tonight? We get to see Anthony's family," I tried to lighten the mood.

I put my hand on his and he pulled it away. He smiles at me and looks out into the pub. I can never tell if it was that he didn't want to be seen holding hands with another man, or if he just didn't want to touch me.

After meeting with Anthony's family in our short time in Belfast, I had begun to notice a shift in Robert's mentality - he was becoming aggressive in conversations. There was a horribly awkward moment when he had blatantly insulted Anthony's father by saying the man didn't understand the dangers of the 5G towers in his own Irish backyard. It was uncomfortable and embarrassing. Was he fatigued or bored by the trip? Why was he all of the sudden so unhappy?

Laying in a hotel bed on our last night in Belfast, I turn and lean into him, I pull myself into the crook of his arm and in the same motion, he moves to sit up. He walks out of the room and to the bathroom. Moving back to my side of the bed, wondering if I should attempt to be close to him again when he returns or not, I begin to cry. Should I be happy that I had a glimpse of hope? That hope, and the joy it brought me, now feels foolish.

***

The night we return to Toronto, we go to Arthur White's apartment for a drink after dinner. Arthur is interested in what we have seen, what the "boys of Ireland" look like. Being a recluse, he lives the fantasy of travel and new places through us. I try and steer the conversation towards the sights, instead of the youthful male population of each city we visited.

"It's just amazing that everyone is so genuinely nice there, I think it ha-"

Robert starts waving his hands at me from the other side of the couch, his sign to me to be quiet.

"We saw this one guy in a bar in Belfast who was playing guitar and singing, he was cute, probably about 22, cute guy" Robert cuts in. Satisfied that he's sold the fantasy, he reclines and sips his cocktail.

There is a careful tension in the room. The conversation moves along.

I can feel Robert showing the signs of being intoxicated next to me.

"There is nothing quite like the Irish hospitality" I attempt to continue "it just seeps into a lot of what they-" Robert takes a loud breath in and starts talking over me.

"We drove through a town called Sneem, I used to bang a guy from Sneem." Another story to elevate his sexual history, to brag about how many guys he's fucked, as if it makes up for being in a long-term relationship now.

"I was still talking," I said sharply.

"Yeh you had your chance to talk, it's the quick and dead around here! If you want to talk, just, have something better than that to say. Arthur doesn't care about your churches and pubs... so anyway," he turned to Arthur, who was looking bug-eyed at the conversation. "I used to bang this guy from Sneem, he was studying at Ryerson I think, he was a good lay."

I decided to stay silent. I sunk lower into the couch. Another act of making myself smaller and quieter.

Walking home from Arthur's apartment, keeping quiet, hands in my pockets and shoulders slumped. I can tell from Robert's breathing and gait, that he wants to argue with me. Giving him nothing in response is my only defence.

Laying down in our king-sized bed, there is enough space to sleep away from each other, uninterrupted by the other's touch. A few feet apart yet completely alone. Temporarily loveless. Again.

CHAPTER 8

The office that my therapist was now operating out of was a multi-use space with private breakout rooms. It was a departure from her well-styled home. It felt more clinical, more serious, colder. There was a waiting room, filing cabinets, and even an old coffee table with obscure magazines on it.

She called me into her breakout room, I walked in hanging my light coat over the chair as I sat down opposite her.

I hadn't sent her any dreams for a few weeks, a prerequisite for most therapists who practise Jungian Analytics. There was a purpose to this, I didn't want her to know how uncomfortable the dreams I was having were. Dreams that I was being killed, dreams of being chased, hunted down. They were becoming so uncomfortably violent that I didn't want to relive them.

"I just haven't had any dreams lately" I lied to my therapist.
"That's Ok, you have been working a lot, why don't we just talk about that. How is the new bar? What is it called?" she queried.

"The new bar is coming along nicely, it's called Beskära. I really like the owner, Matt, he is lovely and very thoughtful. I have known him for about 5 years, he kept telling me he was opening a bar, I guess I just didn't think it would happen this quickly." I stated. Facts. Stick to facts.

"And you are going to keep working at the other bar, Mavericks, right?" she had a concerning look in her eye as she asked.

"Yes, I am going to be at Mavericks a few nights a week and keep my weekend management shifts with them, and work at Beskära during the week. Probably four mornings. It will give me one whole day off and a few long days but other than that, it should all be easy." I confidently said.

"Do you think that might be a bit too much work?" she said, concerned.

"Well, the good thing is that I have the opportunity to recover some of the lost wages and tips from having a broken arm this past winter and not being able to work." Why was I sounding so argumentative?

"Do you think there will be a time that you could go down to just working the one job, or maybe just work a little less? From what you are describing, you are leaving very little time for anything else this summer, would you agree?" she probed again.

"Well, actually..." I was trying to sound less aggressive. "...my schedule would pan out that I have a full day off during the week, and hopefully it coincides with Robert's day off work too. I will also be home five nights a week by 5 pm,, I feel like that is giving me a fair amount of time off. Going to the gym and running will help keep my mind at ease this summer too. I have three marathons planned for the fall, so..." I said, hoping she would move on to another topic.

"From what you have told me about the new bar, the environments seem very different. What is something you think you can gain from the new job?" she asked. I relaxed my face, she had picked up on my stubbornness to think that this much work was a good idea.

"Oh they are like night and day, I mean, roughly the same business idea, they are both breweries. I think the key difference is going to be in the management of them. The owner of Mavericks, Steve, is brash and quite frankly an asshole. Whereas, the owner of Beskära is amazing. It's like night and day." I repeated. I was holding back from telling her that I downright had a crush on Matt. Holding back on telling her the hours I had spent daydreaming about him, fantasizing over what our pillow talk would be, fantasizing over how we would be a power couple in the industry - him, a brewery owner and me, a restaurant manager. Holding back on telling her I had committed every inch of his face to memory.

"Why do you say that about the owner of Mavericks?" she said, pulling me out of thinking about Matt and his perfect face.

"Because it's true," I retorted quickly. "He has no idea what's going on in his own business. And he sits drinking at the bar every night, the man lives off steak and whisky, while trying to run a business. It's a pity because the place is great, and he'd see this if he just got out of there occasionally." I finished.

"If you were to stop working there, would that be so bad?" she asked.

"I mean, the money I make in tips as a floor manager there is great, it's not like I can financially just walk away from a job like that." I responded.

"And you won't earn like that at Beskära?" she queried.

"Who knows? That is the problem with my industry, you can be running a business for someone, but they pay you less than minimum wage because you earn tips. It's a hard situation to be in. On paper, it is a minimum wage job, but if you work hard enough, you can make a great living. It's hard to walk away from that to follow someone else's dream, no matter how you feel about them." I said stopping short at the end.

"How you feel about who's dream? Matt? Do you think he has a good idea for his bar?" she had hit a nerve in me again.

I didn't feel like telling her that I had a deep crush on my new boss and that I was supplementing my relationship with Robert with it. I didn't want to say that every time Robert kissed me, I closed my eyes and thought of Matt.

"He is a lovely guy, as I said. He has been talking about this concept for a while, I have known him for a few years, he… he is very handsome and very thoughtful. He is the type of guy that is very rugged and solid, but also smart, wears glasses when he reads or works on his laptop. Just seems like he has it all together. But also has a small anxiety in his face." I could feel myself saying too much, but I couldn't stop. "He wears soft linen clothes and wants to build an ecologically friendly garden on the roof of the brewery. He wants to train the opening staff in all kinds of soft skills. Matt wants his staff to be enlightened to the nuance of his vision for a responsible business."

She had a suspicious look in her eyes, her body language had shifted on her seat. Could she tell that I had a crush on Matt?

"I think it is safe to say, I am a little infatuated with Matt." I jumped in. outing myself, an act of self-realization.

"Well, it sounds like it is easy to become infatuated by the way you have described him." her eyes becoming momentarily wide, as if we were sharing gossip about a man we both had a crush on. "Is it why you took the job?" she moved on.

"I don't really know. I mean, it could be a factor, but the opportunity is amazing even without his charm. He also hired one of my close friends Lauren to be the general manager, so it is a good fit." I replied.

"Tell me about Lauren," she asked.

"Lauren is great, I have worked for her a lot over the last few years, in different breweries. She is what I aspire to be in our industry. I think I am about two years behind her, professionally. We work well together." I concluded.

"Do you see any parallels between Matt and Robert?" she asked. Did she realize she jolted the conversation?

I was caught off guard. I had not thought about the two of them comparatively.

"Well, they are both tall, both very attractive. But no, I think where Matt is thoughtful and insightful into things in a holistic way, Robert is not. Robert is blunt. Robert has no tact with things, it's part of his charm, his bravado." I blurted out, wishing I said less.

"What do you think a trip like the one you just had with Robert, to Ireland would be like with Matt?" she asked, leaning her head down to write on her notepad. The way she posed the question was so disarming.

"Well, I guess... I think Matt would have done more research into some smaller, more boutique places to visit. Instead of the Guinness brewery, we might have gone to a smaller independent brewery. Maybe have a few meals in some more upscale restaurants, go to a museum or two." I was mumbling my words out of me as I realized how much more I would have preferred the fantasy trip with Matt instead of mediocre meandering with Robert.

"Robert and you didn't go to any museums?" she asked, looking up from her notepad.

"No, he won't set foot in them. Unless a guy around his age and size tells him to. For example, we went to a few places that Anthony recommended, and because Robert has a soft spot for Anthony, we went where he said to go. Except for a few hikes in Belfast, Robert was in a bad mood the last few days of the trip, so we kind of just, went from meal to meal, like boring tourists. But everything we did was recommended by Anthony. Which is fine, I like going to places my friends have enjoyed, but I also like to have some sense of adventure, explore a bit, have my own experiences and just see where I end up. " I said, again, wishing to say less.

"What was Robert in a bad mood about?" she asked.

"It's hard to say." I paused to take a breath. "We were staying with Anthony's uncle, Paul, in Northern Ireland. It was a lovely place, and everything was great, but then Paul's wife Trish started talking about 5G towers and vaccines, and Robert got so engrossed in it, and afterwards, en route to Belfast, I made the mistake of talking to him about it." I said.

"What was there to talk about?" she asked.

"Well, this woman was lovely, but an anti-vaxxer, and was preaching to Robert quite passionately about the health risk, and, well, government mind control through newly installed 5G towers," I said, stirring my hands up in a gesture to indicate the ridiculousness of the issue. "It was very difficult for me not to call her out, I felt deeply conflicted. I just wanted her to stop talking about it, but it's not like you can ask someone to stop talking about something like that in their own house. Plus, she's my friend's uncle's wife, and I didn't want to insult her." I paused for another breath, talking so fast, my thoughts pouring out of my mouth before I could catch them. "Robert is so gullible with these things. He just latches on to them so quickly and then worse, he takes measures to protect himself against whatever threat he's perceived. It is frustrating." I said, starting to focus on anything but the speed in which she was scrawling on her notepad.

There was a small silence between us, just a moment. I hate these moments, I get scared of what she will ask me next.

"It makes me scared of the measures he will go to in order to satisfy his obsession with these conspiracy theories," I continued. "It's like he abandons common sense and acts out of fear of something as stupid as the idea of sinister government mind control. He is afraid that there will be a world war this year, and that there will be no food. So he went out and bought 15 kilos of different dry beans. He doesn't even know how to cook them... He tried to buy cryptocurrency, but when I was helping him do it, I realized he had absolutely no concept of how it worked and was only buying it because of a conspiracy video he saw on YouTube, convincing him that there was about to be a total economic collapse. So I just pretended that I had no idea what to do." I couldn't stop now, as I realized this was actually a bigger problem for me than I'd allowed myself to believe.

"Does his paranoia often affect his mood in things like this?" she asked. Tempting me to say more.

"It's like he loses brain cells just by thinking about these things. He starts to make all these mean comments, and I have to dumb myself down just to avoid an argument. So yeah, when we were in Ireland and that woman said those things, It put him in a totally different headspace. He was really aggressive and kind of frowned for the rest of the trip. And was just plain mean to me." I blurted out, suddenly getting uncomfortable in my seat.

"Are you mean back?" she asked.

"Well, it's... I don't really know how to deal with this behaviour, and it's new! It has only been present in the last few years. He was never like this before. I mean he used to buy a lot of multivitamins, but I took that as self-preservation. He has just become so nihilistic!" I finished. Sitting back and shifting my weight in the armchair. Saying it out loud felt liberating but scary. How could I be with someone like this? Love him? Want to share my life with him, when we had such different outlooks on such fundamental issues?

There was now a welcomed silence between us. She stopped writing on the pad, looked up to me, lowering her glasses.

THE DETERMINIST

"What would you have done if you were in Ireland by yourself?" she asked.

"When I was younger I used to travel a lot by myself, backpacking through cities all over the world. I would always stay in hostels, which always had a few other like-minded people my age to hang out with in each city. I would see how much I could do in a day while spending very little money. I would always try and fit into the place too, dress like a local, walk as if I knew where I was going." I said, deflecting the thought of being alone on travels.

"Do you miss the way you used to travel?" she asked, obviously not letting me off the hook.

"It was fun, I used to run most mornings while I was travelling. I would go to cities just to run marathons. I would plan weeks of travel around running marathons. For example, I went to Europe for three months at one point, stayed with a cousin in Paris, but ran four marathons in different cities in France, Holland and Germany. I'd go on dates with guys I'd meet either at hostels or in gay bars. Life was good and easy. I had money from working in resorts in the summer. I had some real passion about me then." I trailed off. Remembering all the feelings of excitement about the world I used to have. Where did it go? Could I get it back? Did I want it back?

"What are some of the differences you see in how you travel now?" she continued.

"Well, now it's different, it's compromising. He doesn't want to come along to marathon weekends, so I normally just drive to the race and return after I am finished. But when we travel together there is a lot of travelling by car, which I never would have done when I was younger, bus was my preferred method. Or train. I would travel extremely light, I could fit six weeks of things into a small backpack, do laundry once every few weeks, shower in my running clothes to clean them. I would meet new people all the time in hostels, sometimes I wouldn't even have a plan for where I was going, just land somewhere with some vague idea of where I wanted to go. I was intrepid. Robert likes to have everything planned out, every route needs to be studied, he has to figure out which hotel will be most comfortable in a small town, which beach to go to. It was a learning curve for me, and him too. He hadn't left North America when we met. Our first trip internationally was to Australia for my brother's wedding. He had no concept of proper travel. The realities of lining up at airports, being ok with not having a solid meal for a while. He never wanted to stay in a hostel. We always stayed in hotels. It felt unnecessary spending all that money, but it was a way to get him to come." I realized that I had now been talking for roughly five minutes without taking a breath, and most of what I was saying was being scribed down on a notepad.

Taking a short breath, I tilted my head. Waiting for her to stop scribbling down everything that was flowing out of my mouth...

"I guess it's just different when you travel with someone else," I concluded, hoping that was a big realization.

She finally stopped writing, looked up to me and locked eyes.

"How long did it take Robert to get out of the bad mood he was in Belfast?" she asked, fixing her gaze on me.

"Well, he hasn't really, we have been home for two weeks and he's still acting aloof. I am about to start working one of the busiest summers I have had in years, and he is just kind of shut off to me, he won't talk about anything serious." I said with an air of defeat.

"How long do these bouts tend to last?" she asked, still not lowering her gaze.

"Well, normally it all either peters itself out over a week, then he focuses on something else for a while. But there is the possibility that we fight, things get pretty heated, and the only way to get him out of the hangover of the fight is for me to concede and say sorry to him." I said, flatly.

"And is that when the bargaining starts from him?" she said.

I was taken aback. I had told her about this pattern in a previous session but didn't expect her to remember it that well. Was this pattern and its outcome something she noted before as a problem?

"I guess so. The last time it was about my body, he told me I had put on weight and that I was moody" I said. Looking down at my shoes, I realized that shame was becoming a regular feeling in therapy.

"So what was the bargaining about this time?" she asked.

"That's just it. He is still in this weird mood. I can't get a read on him. He is obviously depressed. And it's not like he can call me fat right now. I have kept myself this thin for months. So I'd like to see what he tries to blame it on this time" I blurted out. Feeling lightheaded by the shock of what I had just said.

There was another silence in the room. I put my head forward, I felt like crying but no tears were coming out. My chin started trembling.

"I don't know what I'm doing wrong. I cannot get it right with him. He won't go to see a couple's therapist together. I just hate feeling like I am constantly defeated by this relationship." I said.

"Why won't he see a couples therapist?" she asked.

"I think he is afraid because it is easier to blame the failures on me. I pointed this out to him. But he just said it was stupid. It's like he knows he is doing things that are going to affect our relationship badly but he does them anyway, and then has this look on his face as if he has done something wrong and is trying to justify it. Or worse, make it my fault."

"What are the bad things he is doing?" she asked, she could tell I had revealed something I didn't want to.

I took a moment to bring myself together, breathing, feeling the weight of what I was finally about to put into words.

"He knows I know about the cheating. I know that he is seeing at least two other guys regularly. I mean, we agreed on an open relationship, but sex only, nothing else. He knows I know about this one guy that it's obvious he really likes. His name is Clayton." I said.

"How do you know about this person?" she asked.

"We share a laptop. It's an Apple and it is connected to his iPhone. So when he gets a message on his phone and I am on the computer, it dings up on the messages, on the corner of the screen." I flatly revealed. I hadn't told anyone this. I barely wanted to acknowledge it myself.

"Did you confront him about this?" she asked.

"Yeah, he said it was just sexual. I reminded him that we had agreed not to hide things and that he and I hadn't had sex in months. He said he wouldn't want to have sex with me because I had been moody and grumpy-looking. It was a really bad day. I went to sleep in the second room, but he came and got me and brought me to our bed, and said he was sorry, and then we held each other crying. It was really bad." Another moment I'd wanted to forget, revealed.

"Do you ever act on the agreement?" she asked.

"I used to, sometimes when I was working a lot on the other side of town. But I wouldn't go out of my way. We started it because he told me he couldn't have as much sex as I wanted to have. He made it sound like it was solely for my benefit. I agreed, thinking it would be progressive and liberating. It just made me feel like shit, to be honest." I admitted

"There are a lot of gay couples that have similar arrangments, but they seem to be based on trust. Would you say you trust Robert?" she asked, staring intently at me.

I looked at the clock on the wall, our session was close to ending.

"I am committed to our relationship. I need help figuring out how to make this work. It's getting rough and I need better tools to make this work" I said defensibly.

"Yes, I understand that," she said, raising her hand to cut me short... "But I am asking is, do you trust Robert in your relationship?"

I could feel myself getting more upset. I could feel the discomfort in what she had just said. It sat, taking up space between us. It felt like both of us were unsure about where my answer would take us.

"I don't know," I said, defusing the comment. "But I do know that I care about fixing this relationship. And I am working towards it, I just have to figure out a way to get through to him. I love him. He is understanding if I just talk to him about how I feel." It was like I was pleading with her to give me the magic answer that would bring back the man I was in love with.

"Have you done this before with him?" she probed, with the tone of a knowing mother scolding a child.

"Yeah, we normally have a routine where we have the talk, but then something in the relationship is damaged for a few months, and I get really insecure about it and think I have done something wrong. So I apologize, and he gets to feel like Alpha once more and starts treating me kindly again. So it just seems to be this messed up way of working." I said bringing the conclusion of the topic.

"Look, Greg, we are going to have to leave it there, but I think this has been one of our most productive sessions in a long time," she said, sitting forward on her chair and placing her notepad back onto the coffee table.

"Yeah, I think so too." I agreed, collecting myself. "See you again this time next week?"

"Yes, and don't worry about the dreams, they will come when they are supposed to, you just need to spend some time figuring out how you are going to achieve some of these goals you have set for yourself with work." She ended on a practical note as if to tie off the open nerves she'd just exposed.

"Yeah, right, ok. I'll see you next week" I said, standing up out of the chair.

I started putting my coat on as I was leaving the office, making my way down the hallway. I stood in front of the elevator about to cry.

Looking behind me, I slipped into the staircase before the elevator doors opened and took a few flights down, trying to stop myself from crying. In defeat, I sat down on the cold concrete step and clutched the railing. A loud, sob came out of me. Hot tears fell down my cheeks and tasted salty. My shoulders shook as I surrendered to the moment, and hoped no one would need the stairs and interrupt my release.

It was a few minutes before I heard the door a few floors above me open and fast-paced steps start to rumble down the staircase. I quickly collected myself off the step and started down the stairs.

Opening the door to the lobby, I tried to nod at the security guard but ended up just looking at the ground.

Outside, the traffic of the night was welcoming. It was past twilight and the evening was settling in. Making the small walk home from the office building, I started preparing myself to walk back into our home. I could see Robert through the kitchen window as I moved towards the front door, sitting at the laptop reading. I fumbled my keys to get into the house.

As soon as I was through the door, I heard him let out a yawn and say "Greg?" in a playful tone.

"Just a second, got to use the washroom, I'll be up in a second," I called out.

I went to the lower level bathroom, standing in front of the vanity, I turned the tap on. I splashed some water on my face. Some of it went down my collar onto my chest, making a mark on my shirt. I rubbed my eyes and turned the tap off. Wiping down my face, I left the bathroom to climb the stairs to the kitchen.

Robert was sitting just how I had seen him through the window.

"Hey, bud!" Robert said, with a happy and light tone to his voice. He turned around to look at me. Seeing that my face and eyes were red, he got up out of his seat and moved towards me.

"Are you ok? Hey, hey, what's wrong?" he asked with a consoling tone.

He drew me into a hug and I tried to tell him that I had just washed my face. I nuzzled my face into the crook of his chest and tilted my head up to kiss him. He responded and put a hand on my lower back.

"You're ok bud, you're ok," he said again. "What's wrong, huh? What's wrong?" he continued. It felt nice, it felt like he cared.

We stayed in an embrace for another moment, I was crying and there was no hiding it. He grabbed me by the shoulders and sat me down at the kitchen table. Turning to the fridge he opened it and passed me a beer, and sat down across from me.

"What is happening bud? You had a hard session?" he asked again.

Why was he all of the sudden being so considerate of me? I had walked into this house ready to have a conversation about his behaviour over the last two weeks, but now I am completely disarmed by him. Everything that was on my mind from the therapy session to now was dissolving. The carefully thought-out words I would use to engage him in a constructive conversation were jumbled again. Did he know this? Sense it somehow? Was the purpose of the kindness to disarm me? He looked into my eyes and put his hands on my chin. Pulled me into another kiss.

"I just get so scared sometimes" I finally let out.

"Oh, buddy. Scared of what?" he said, pulling me into another embrace.

"Scared that you are going to leave me soon. It's just been so hard over the last few weeks." I said. I took a sip from the beer he had handed me.

"Oh buddy, I love you, we are in this together. Don't worry about all that stuff. Hey, c'mon, you're ok..." he said in a consoling tone. Was it consoling or condescending?

I hadn't cried to him like this before, I guess this was my shot.

"I just get scared that I am not making you happy, and that you want out, and I am doing all that I can to be what you want, it's just so hard. I feel horrible half the time because of this." I confessed to him.

He pulled me into a tighter embrace and held me for a moment.

"I love you buddy, I don't want to see you crying like this," he said wiping a tear off my face and softly smiling at me.

"I love you too, I just get so scared." I retorted.

"Hey hey hey, c'mon now you don't need to be scared. We are fine, I am not going anywhere," he said. Looking at me and holding my hands in his.

"Okay," I mumbled out. "I think I just got a little overwhelmed," choking my tears down.

Taking a moment to bring my breath back to normal, we took small sips of beer. We sat in the kitchen waiting for the emotion to wash past me.

"Buddy, you don't need to worry, I am not going anywhere." Robert finally said after another embrace.

Maybe this is it. We had never cried like this together over something like this. I was just so upset and confused.

"Why don't you go take a shower and calm down a bit, and I'll go to the falafel place and grab some dinner for us, you want to do that?" he said in an almost playful tone. In the wrong light, he could be seen as condescending, but I accept this as a genuine gesture.

I make my way upstairs to the shower as he leaves to go to fetch dinner for us. Taking my clothes off in front of the mirror, I look at my reflection. My eyes were puffy and my mouth turned down in the corners. I took a breath in, the type that shudders after you have been crying. Stepping into the shower, feeling the warm water run over me, I start to feel better. He loves me and I love him. I can make it work. I just need to try a little harder.

CHAPTER 9

Beskära had been open for 6 weeks. The pride I felt from being a part of such a successful restaurant open was sustaining. Work at Mavericks was just as hectic as every other summer. I was barely at home. My weeks had started to have a good rhythm. I was working at Beskära four mornings a week as the opening manager and at Mavericks two nights as a closing manager, and two brunch shifts as a manager. During my off time, I was going to the gym and training for the marathons planned for the end of the summer.

Robert seemed happy enough, it was obvious that he was still seeing his boyfriend Clayton. It bothered me, but if it is what it took to keep this relationship surviving, then it's what needed to happen. The pain of it all was bringing out some good results for me in the gym. I was lythe and strong. My body was responding to multiple stresses well, despite the nights I wasn't able to sleep. Nights spent staring at Robert while he slept. Wondering what would happen if I just got up and left in the middle of the night.

Caroline had been living in Manhattan on and off over the last few years for work. Every few months either I would go to New

York or she would come to Toronto. One day when I was on my way to the gym after work, Caroline called me.

"So, I know you are super busy, but I just want to come up for a visit and see you before I head back to Australia. I just want to get into nature," she said over the phone.

I cleared my schedule for the few days that she was coming, rented a car and booked an Airbnb spot along the Georgian Peninsular. I felt like it would be impressive to take her to the bars in Toronto I had put so much time and effort into, and show her what I had been doing for the last few months.

Robert told me he wouldn't have time off work to come with us on our getaway. I knew that it would only upset his work schedule by one day, which would be easy to move around for him. As he told me I had a pit in my stomach, knowing that for the nights I was gone, Clayton or some other adulterer would be in my bed, in such close proximity to the comforts of my personal life. It made me feel sick in the stomach to think about.

Over the few weeks leading to Caroline arriving, there was a stage of emotional standoff between Robert and I. The promises of the prior month felt long gone, forgotten. It did not feel like we were ok. He was becoming more and more distant, and I was becoming more and more frustrated.

One afternoon Anthony and I were sitting in the back garden, listening to music and catching up over a few beers, a sad song came on over the playlist, Anthony halted what he was saying, turned to me and said;

"This song takes me back, it was my sad song that got me through the breakup with Kathleen."

"It's a good song," I replied.

"Maybe it will be your breakup song…" he said, going a shade of pale as he realized what he had said. "… I mean, your carry on song, the song that gets you through the next few months," he concluded.

I looked at him almost exacerbated, then took a sip of my beer and chuckled.

"God you are dramatic, not everyone needs to break up," I replied, feeling like I had successfully diffused the comment on his behalf.

***

The ease in which Caroline and I had always talked to each other was being tested. I hated lying to her. I could keep my issues with Robert hidden from everyone else, but it felt like a betrayal hiding it from her. Since we were young, she would always look out for me. She stood up to schoolyard bullies teasing me for being an effeminate boy, agreed with me on issues fought over at the family dinner table. She was my protector, and not telling her about the issues, was the first time I had kept something like this from her. I was starting to think she would see right through me.

Caroline's plane was to land at 5 pm on a Friday, just as I was finishing work, and we had planned to meet at a bar near my home. I hadn't checked my phone while working, but when I returned to my office from the barroom floor, my phone blinked at me. Caroline had sent me a slew of texts.

11.05 am Got off work early, going to see if I can get the earlier flight'

11.38 am 'on way to the airport, hopefully, I can get the earlier flight, will put me in downtown at around 3'

12.24 pm 'just boarded the flight! Bottle of duty-free gin in hand! Land at 1.45, will head to the house'

1.38 pm 'landed early, haven't heard anything from you, just going to head over to yours and maybe jump over the back fence or something lol'

2.25 pm 'just text Robert, he is going to meet me once he finishes up at hockey practice! See you when you finish work'

I had a pang of panic, what if Robert told her that we are having problems, what if she catches on quickly and has already made up her mind about what is going on? What if I get home and he has told her that I have been depressed and kind of shut off?

I finish up my work quickly and head to the front of the restaurant, having the small chats that you need to have when passing off a shift for a busy Friday night. I made my way out to my bike, it was such a hot day that my bike seat was uncomfortably hot to sit on. Riding home, I was excited to see Caroline, but also a small pit of fear was in my stomach. What if she saw right through me the minute she laid eyes on me?

I got home, while putting my bike in the garage I took a moment to catch myself. I walked into the front door of the house. I could hear Robert and Caroline in the back garden.

"Greg?" Robert called out.

"Hi, I'm coming!" I replied. Startled by the moment, my protective sister and my difficult partner.

Making my way out to the back garden I see the makeshift bar sitting on the coffee table, a sizable amount of gin was missing from the new bottle. Sliced lemons and empty cans of tonic water littered the small table. I stepped out into the garden. The plants in the garden were fragrant this time of night, and seeing Caroline smiling up at me from the other side of the table was enough to make me forget about all the troubles I had been having over the last few months.

"Hey kid!" she said as she rose from her chair to pull me into a hug. "My god you are sweaty!" she exclaimed.

After a few minutes of small talk, I rested my seat on the arm of Robert's chair and he put his arm around my lower back and pulled me down to kiss and say hello. I felt relieved that we could appear to be a normal, affectionate couple for a moment.

Realizing they were both a little tipsy from the gin. I excused myself to have a quick shower. While preparing for the shower, I smiled at myself in the mirror. He was being kind to me in front of my sister. All my hard work is starting to pay off.

I returned to the garden, it was dusk and Robert had lit candles. The garden I had built was abundant in greenery, there were blue hostas', a pink hydrangea, and a curtain of tiger lilies in the back. The ambience was calming. After weeks of business, I finally felt some calm come over me. Caroline smiled at me, Robert made jokes. I prepared a salad in the kitchen while Caroline and Robert turned sausages on the grill. It was becoming a perfect summer night.

After dinner was done and the night drew to a close, Robert and I ascended to the master bedroom together. Brushing our teeth in the mirror and smiling at our reflections. I hadn't seen him with a sparkle in his eye for years. It was working. What I was doing was saving us.

We got into bed, trying not to push my luck, I lay on my side like we normally slept. He reached over to me and grabbed me by the shoulder and pulled me into his naked body, his intentions clear to me. After contemplations of whether or not Caroline's sleep would be disturbed, we slowly and quietly started making love. Or at least some version of shared intimacy. I fell asleep afterwards feeling like I had fixed the fracture. He was in love with me again. I had done it. Success.

Robert woke me up as he was leaving by kissing me on the cheek.

"Have a good day bud," he whispered to me before he left.

***

Through the first part of the week, Caroline and I had made the most of the hours I wasn't at work, and it was fun taking her to some cool new bars around the city, meeting with some of my friends that had also become hers in Toronto. Robert was in good spirits. He was beginning to show signs of affection again. I found my spirits lifting. He even came up behind me and kissed my neck when I was preparing dinner one night.

When I was at work, away from him and away from the reality of the relationship, I felt uneasy. There was a pit in my stomach of anxiety, twisting and turning throughout the day.
I finally sent a text to Robert.

'Are you sure you don't want to come with us up north this weekend?' I sent him.

Arriving home late that night from work, the house was still. Robert was asleep, Caroline's door was shut. The bottle of gin looked almost empty. I slowly made my way to bed, it wasn't long until I had to get up to go back to work. All this work made me fall asleep in seconds.

Robert woke me up with a nudge.

"Hey, your alarm didn't go off, you... have work right?" he asked.

Sitting bolt upright, I was startled by the time. By my calculation, I had 15 minutes to shower, have breakfast, and leave for work. I despise being woken up like this or being rushed in the morning.

"Why didn't you wake me up sooner?" I asked Robert.

"You have time to get ready, you're fine, you just looked so peaceful asleep like that," he replied sounding sinister but at the same time sweet.

I jumped out of the bed and into the bathroom. I splashed water onto my face and started brushing my teeth. As I was doing so I started changing into fresh clothes.

"Aren't you going to shower?" Robert called out.

I ignored what he was saying and carried on. I needed to get out of this house, quickly and efficiently. Rinsing the last of the toothpaste foam from my mouth I washed my face again in the sink.

"I just don't have time. I am running late now," I called out to Robert.

Passing him in the bedroom I knelt in for a kiss, he was looking at his phone. I tried not to notice that he was on Grindr. We were on such a good streak.

"Did you think about what I asked you yesterday? Do you think you will be able to make it up north with us?" I asked in a calmer tone than what my actions had been.

"Not possible bud, I have work on Saturday then I'm playing the final hockey game for the summer series on Sunday. Got stuff planned," he replied with an annoyed look on his face.

It took a great deal of energy not to ask how long after I had left would Clayton be coming in for the weekend. I grinned through the moment. Stifling myself down again. I leaned in and kissed him.

"See you tonight, love you," I said as I was leaving him.
"Love you too bud, have a good day," he replied.

***

Caroline was impressed with the number of cars that were heading north on the 400. I had just finished a hard day at Beskära, where Matt and Lauren were in a panic about the executive chef. After a few weeks of what seemed like differing opinions and small fights, had turned into a type of cold war between management and the kitchen. Losing control of your kitchen at any stage for an owner is a tough position, never mind it happening in the first two months of opening. After some sharp conversations, the chef had quit and started making plans to take staff with her. It was creating a lot of stress in the management team. Even more little intense conversations in hallways, more deciding words. Not the ideal time to be saying, 'well, off to cottage country for the weekend, bye!' Matt and Lauren assured me that it would be fine.

"Are we going to listen to Fleetwood Mac the whole trip?" Caroline piped up.

"Oh no I just turned on what I thought was going to be good highway vibes. Put on whatever you want" I said gesturing to my phone in the console. "The password is 2204."

Caroline opened the phone and started navigating towards the playlists, jumbling through them. A beep came over the speaker, alerting the arrival of a text message.

"Oh it's from Robert, he wrote 'have a good time with your sister, we can talk more about what we said last night.' "yikes," she continued to look at my phone. "What happened last night?" she concluded.

I hadn't told Caroline about the sharp conversations I had had with Robert after she had gone to bed the night before. Robert had started cleaning up the bedroom, which was in a state of slight mess from me packing up clothes for the weekend away. He started to grab my things and put them in draws haphazardly. I had asked him to stop and that I would tidy up when I got home from the trip. He told me that he wanted the place tidy before

I left. I asked him why it was so important. I knew why. He was having someone else over for the weekend. The truth that I knew hung in the air between us that night.

"Oh nothing, ...we were discussing a trip this winter." I lied to Caroline.

She gave me a suspicious look. "Ok," she said.

She can tell when I am lying. I don't know how she knows, but she does. She somehow knows the reason for the lie is important to me, so she doesn't always push me for the truth.

After a few hours of driving we arrived at a cottage I had rented in a small town. It was a 20-minute walk to the pub down the street, where I had planned to have a pint to kick off the little getaway. We dropped our bags off and walked down the street as twilight approached us. As we walked, I started to open up to Caroline about what had happened at work. She knew how much I had put into the opening of Beskära, with little chance of much professional advancement.

"It's just so unfair of this chef to do this, like we all worked so hard on the open to have a successful offering in the restaurant, and she is taking all that away. It is just so severe. So rude," I said at the end of explaining the situation.

"Oh, well you know, sometimes someone is just unhappy in the role they are in and they know they cannot give it their best," she said. I glanced at her as she said it. I knew she knew something. She was being too diplomatic, I just needed her to say that this chef was terrible.

"Yeah, but when you start something like that, something as personal as a small business for a hard-working, independent guy who just wants good things for the entire team, it just fucking sucks. The nerve of them, the whole kitchen team to have this... this coup. It's just so wrong. We built a whole program around this chef and now, six weeks in, the chef is going to walk away and try and take half the kitchen team with her. It's just fucked." I carried on.

"Yeah, it sucks," she replied.

We walked up to the pub in the center of the town. Walking in I noticed the population of the bar was mainly older, portly country folk. Everyone seemed cheery and relaxed, no one looked up to notice us enter the bar, something that happens in most Toronto bars. We sat at the counter. Looking out over the bottles lining the walls of the bar, I began to become impatient after just one minute.

"Man, there isn't even anyone tending this bar," I said quietly to Caroline.

"Oh give it a minute. I know you like to judge every other bar to the ones you are used to, but this is not your bar, just be nice." she retorted.

I was slightly taken back, was Caroline used to my behaviour being slightly rude? But she was right, every time I walked into a dining room or bar, I would start judging the layout, the menu, the service, the food... I was pedantic.

A smiley bartender approached us and took our order.

"You know, the long game professionally is more about how you can problem solve the issues like this that come up. You don't have to respond to all of them with such anger." Caroline said after her first sip of wine.

"I get it, but it just sucks, it feels like a betrayal," I replied.

"I just think that it is amazing that you have this passion for this, but at the end of it, the bar is going to get through it, it has so many other things to offer with the brewery and the garden space. There are going to be other chefs out there that can take over, and who knows, maybe do it better. I think that another chef that will dedicate themselves to the establishment might be a better fit," Caroline finished.

I stayed silent, stewing in panic. She had caught on. There is no way she wasn't using this as a metaphor.

The bartender dropped off our dinner. I was surprised by the meal, it was delicious and a little out of character for the pub and location. We ordered more drinks after we had finished eating. I was starting to feel the tension in my back dissipate. Caroline was giggly and starting to yawn. Telling her what had been happening between Robert and I would have to wait until the morning.

***

"Love the smell of pine trees!" Caroline said at our first beach stop.

I looked around at the birch, the maple, the oak trees that surrounded the small lakefront beach we were about to set up camp for the day.

"There is no pine around us... what is that?" I replied, cut off by the view of Caroline pulling a large, iridescent shawl out of her bag.

"It's my 'going to the beach' shawl, it makes me feel more like a mermaid, and makes me feel prettier in front of the fucking pine trees." She said matter of factly.

There was no denying that Caroline has style, a careful collection of things that look like they were made specifically for her. She had comfort and glamour at the center of everything she wore. Even her pyjamas had small rose gold prints of crowns.

We sat out on the beach and dipped into the water periodically. Conversation flowed around our family. One of the benefits of coming from such a large family, there is always gossip.

"They just seem so unhappy together, it would be better if they just broke up," Caroline said, talking about one of our cousins and his wife. "I mean it's different when you have kids, but I just don't know how she can stand him, he cheated on her while she was home with the babies every night... With the fucking secretary, so typical. It's 2019, people should just be better than this." she continued.

"Well sometimes people are willing to put in the effort and work in the relationship to make it successful, maybe that is what she is doing," I replied in a low voice.

"Yeah, but like, if everyone knew that he was doing it, and it was so obvious, enough people would help her through it. It might be hard to do with a one-year-old, but imagine how hard it would be to raise a kid with someone you don't trust." Caroline continued.

"I don't think it's that simple, a marriage is nuanced and private. There are so many factors that lead to infidelity. I mean if he was out in a bar every night looking to sleep with every woman in sight as his wife was home with the baby, it would be different. He may have had a struggle by falling for his secretary..." I said.

"You cannot seriously defend him in this. Greg, his wife had just had their second baby, and he was habitually sleeping with his secretary, and it's not like the secretary didn't know he had a wife and kid. I bet he spun her a lie too, told her that he was going to leave his wife for her. Typical." Caroline replied.

Why was I defending the actions of my cousin's infidelity? I could feel my neck getting tighter, all the relaxation of the morning starting to give away to the anxious lump in my throat, the pit in my stomach infecting me with despair.

"I just think that sometimes marriage hits a rough patch for some reason and that it sucks but if you have made a promise to someone, and you trust in the fact that you love each other, you can fix things," I said softly, calmly.

Caroline got up and walked into the lake without saying anything to me. I turned onto my stomach and looked up at the trees. Swaying into different directions, there was no doubt that this was a beautiful day. I normally am not one to sit out in the sun all day, but it felt nice to stop and relax. While gazing at the treeline, I wondered if Robert would even have the polite forethought to change our bedsheets before and after his boyfriend was coming to stay.

I rolled onto my back and rose from the beach to enter the water. Caroline was standing out in the shallows, looking out into the lake. I made my way to her.

"I don't think there is anything right in cheating," I said to her when I had finally caught up. "It's just that sometimes, people are in really difficult situations and it makes it very hard to know what to do." I continued.

Carlone sighed with a long exhale. "What are you telling me?" she asked. Not able to look at me in the eyes.

She knew.

"Robert has been having an affair for the last few months. It's different from when we used to have a bit of fun with other guys, he is in a full-on relationship with another guy, well, at least one that I know of." I confessed.

Caroline sighed again. And started to sniffle.

"How long have you known?" she asked.

"About seven weeks. I was going to confront him about it but, I had to open a restaurant. It's been hectic ever since. I just thought if I could make him feel better and be more romantic he would end it with the other guy." I said, realizing how stupid it was as I said it.

"Oh shit Greg, I am so sorry" she replied. "What are you going to do about it?" she asked.

"I'm going to fix it. He had to outsource love, he wasn't getting it from me. I think I need to work less and focus on us, go back to basics," I said half-heartedly.

"Do you think that will work?" Caroline asked.

"I don't know," I replied.

We got out of the lake. We walked to the car as the sun started to set.

"Thank you for telling me this, I know it cannot have been easy," Caroline said as we sat into the car.

"It's going to be a difficult year, but I'll get through it. Promise you won't tell anyone?" I replied a strange hot feeling behind my ears was arriving.

"Of course not, and I know you know, but you can always talk to me about these things. I get it. I understand." Caroline said.

We drove back to the cabin. Caroline poured two glasses of wine as I built a small campfire. We sat gossiping about the family again. I felt as if a weight had been lifted from my chest.

Watching the night approach, I heard my phone buzz.

'Night buddy, hope you had a good day with Caroline, a pretty boring night here.' Robert had texted me.

I wanted to throw my phone into the campfire. I knew he was texting me while probably lying in my bed with someone young and unsuspecting. I felt a rush of anger.

"I don't know what to do most of the time... do you think anyone does?" I asked Caroline, slurring my words.

"Oh god no, most of us just react. It's the only human nature we can rely on," she replied.

After taking the last sip of wine, I told Caroline it was time for me to go to bed. She poured some water on the fire, extinguishing the flames, signalling to the night that we were done. The air suddenly damp around us. Different noises coming from the trees. As we turned towards the house, she pulled me into a hug.

"You're going to be OK kid," she said in a soft and comforting tone.

"I know. I hope so." I replied.

CHAPTER 10

In the weeks following Caroline's visit, I found myself shutting down more. At work, I was starting to find it harder to make my smile seem genuine. Robert had stopped kissing me on the cheek in the morning when he was leaving for work, stopped texting me during the day. He was coming home later than normal and telling me it was because his work was just too busy. I wanted to believe him.

I made sure the fridge was full of food, that dinners were cooked and that the house was clean. Working as many hours as I did, still finding time to get to the gym and do training runs for my marathons, which were now 2 months away.

September came fast. One night Robert and I decided to head to our favourite pub for dinner. On arrival, we found the pub to be closed for the night due to a plumbing issue. There were a few similar pubs in the area, so finding an alternative wouldn't be a problem.

"Where do you want to go?" Robert asked me.

"I don't mind, why don't you choose?" I replied.

"No, where do *you* want to go?" he said more sternly, pointing a finger onto my chest.

"Rob, I don't want to become one of those couples that fight about where to go for dinner, just pick somewhere and we will go," I said, smiling at him.

I leaned in to kiss him on the cheek but he pulled away.

"Why won't you just tell me where you want to go?" he said angrily.

"I don't care where we go, I want to have a nice dinner and a pint. Just pick somewhere buddy," I replied, trying to keep my voice light.

He turned and started walking down the street back towards home. I followed him.

"Robert, where are you going?" I asked.

"I'm going the fuck home" he replied.

We arrived home in silence. I had started to cry on the short walk.

"You are not fucking crying again are you?" Robert said as we walked into the house.

I sniffled trying to stifle my sobs. There was no holding them back. I was tired and upset. He pulled me into a hug.

THE DETERMINIST

"You don't have to be so argumentative all the time buddy, you sometimes just have to tell me what you want instead of starting a fight," Robert said.

We made our way upstairs to the kitchen and assembled a small dinner out of leftovers from the fridge. While preparing our meals, Robert opened up the laptop. As he did, his phone buzzed. The laptop iChat opened a small tile in the top right corner of the screen. He wasn't fast enough to pull it away. There it was. A picture of who I can only imagine to be his boyfriend, naked and bent over, exposing himself to the camera. "Can't wait to see you tomorrow big guy," the text read.

I pretended not to see it. I was standing behind him. He wouldn't know if I had or hadn't seen it. I stood steady in shock, continuing to prepare the food. Feeling the surge of emotions running through me, like a power grid close to failure.

Taking the time to sit down next to him. He looked pale and had a hand over his mouth.

"What's up? I asked, trying not to sound like I was angry.

"Nothing, just reading about the housing bubble," he said back to me. The screen sitting at the top of an article, only a small amount of text at the bottom of the page. Had he been staring at the headline and picture for five whole minutes?

We ate mostly in silence. After cleaning up the kitchen, I made my way upstairs, and from what I could tell, he was now texting someone, probably his boyfriend. I could hear the buzzer going off every few minutes.

Feeling numb, I put myself to bed and pretended to be asleep when he came in.

***

I woke up five minutes before my alarm, Robert was still asleep. I sat watching him sleep for a few moments. The feeling of pain in my chest was beginning to grow again. I went through the motions of my morning routine, coffee, shower, and checking emails on my phone.

Before I left I sat down on Robert's side of the bed, as he was waking up. He normally would have been getting ready for work too but was taking the day off work. It was his hockey league's final summer game, they had made it to the championship of their league. It was a big deal to him.

He lay in bed watching me get dressed. I sat down on his side of the bed, picked up his hands and fell into his blue-eyed gaze.

"Ok, I'm off, I love you, buddy, good luck today, I'll see if I can get out of work early to make it to your game, I'll text you… I love you…" I said and leaned in to kiss him.

"I love you too, and don't worry about the game. It's not a big deal," he replied.

"It is a big deal! And it sounds like fun." I said, getting up from sitting next to him. "Bye, buddy," I said as I walked towards the door.

THE DETERMINIST

The short ride to work was nice, it was the time of year when summer was really settling in. Hot mornings, stuffy nights. Every time I turned in a bike lane, my inner mind went straight to the image I had seen on the computer the night before. It kept winding its way into every thought, obscuring the tasks in front of me.

Opening Beskära for the morning, I was on autopilot. My mind was sitting on the computer screen, the image of that young man burned into my mind's eye.

Staff started to arrive as I was finishing my daily setup. I didn't even pretend to have a warm demeanour. I just wanted to get the day done so I could go home and sleep off this trance I had been in all morning.

Service started for brunch, it was off to a slow start. Lauren dropped into the restaurant.
"How's it going?!" she said energetically.
"Good, I just feel a little unwell, I just... I have something on my mind." I replied.

Lauren and I had been close friends for years, we had worked shoulder to shoulder, helping each other out when we needed it.
"Wanna take the rest of the day off?" she asked, with a concerned look.

I felt instantly guilty, I was letting my personal life seep into my professional life. Something I had strived against. I felt a pang of opportunity in my mind. Maybe going to Robert's hockey game this afternoon would be good for us as a couple, he would know how dedicated I was to him. It would prove to him that I am willing and able to fix this, and yes there would be a hard conversation to have about the fact that he was lying to me, and that he was cheating. If I could just prove to him that I am all in... that I am enough.

"Yeah, I'm so sorry, yeah." I stuttered nervously. I felt tears forming in my eyes.

"Go on! I got this Greg." Lauren said with a reassuring smile.

I made my way to the office to collect my things. I sent a text to Robert telling him that we were in luck and that I was going to make it to his game.

As I was leaving, I checked in again with Lauren. "Are you sure this is ok?" I asked.

"Sure! We will be fine. Text me later if you want to talk." she replied.

Leaving the bar, I got on my bike and started making my way home.

Stopping at a light, I checked my phone. 'Oh don't worry about the game, take the afternoon off. What time are you going to be home?' Robert had replied.

'I am just leaving work now' I texted him.

'I just left for the rink, the game is not for another hour or so, really don't come to the rink, it will be boring for you' he texted back.

I put the phone in my pocket, this was a good plan, I was going to surprise him by being there. Show him how much I cared.

THE DETERMINIST

I turned the corner onto my street. And arrived home. Putting my bike away, I walked up into the kitchen. I was going to have a light lunch, change, and make my way over to the rink. I made myself a sandwich and sat in front of the computer, opening it to find something to entertain me while I ate. I loaded a news stream and bit into my sandwich.

The iChat blinked in the corner.

I knew I shouldn't open it. I hated that I was invading his privacy again, something I had told myself not to do. I sat waging war with myself for a minute.

I pushed my half-eaten sandwich to the side, drawing the MacBook closer to me.

With the mouse hovering over the iChat icon, I took a deep breath and opened the tab.

An active chat was happening between Robert and Clayton. I scrolled down until I reached where I had seen the picture the night before.

Robert 9.45 pm -'Looking good buddy, can't wait to dive into you tomorrow. Just had another fight with my partner so you will be getting the full force of that tomorrow.'

Clayton 9.48 pm' night big guy, see you at the rink tomorrow'

Robert 11.30 am 'so tough news, my partner is getting off work and coming to see me at the rink, I'll try and get him not to come, but if he does, I'll ditch him afterwards and come and meet you'

Clayton 11.34 am 'can I come and watch you anyway, I won't talk to him or you, I just want to watch you play...'

Robert 11.36 am ' Sure... nothing wrong with that...I can't say what time I will be able to come to you this afternoon. But I am definitely coming'

Clayton 11.38 am ' what time is the game again?'

Robert 11.45 am '1.30 pm, just don't talk to my friends you met, Greg will probably be with them, but don't want an awkward situation.'

Clayton 11.51 'got it, see you later on, good luck in the game. See you later sexy'

I felt like I might be sick. I walked to the fridge and got a beer. I drank half the can standing in front of the open fridge. I grabbed another beer, closed the fridge and walked downstairs into the back garden. I texted Anthony as I opened the second beer.

'What are you doing? I need to have a few beers' I text him.
'Was thinking the same thing bro,' he promptly texted back.

We met at a bar near my house.

"What's wrong?" he said before he had even sat down.
"Nothing!" I quickly replied. I started to relax my face.

We talked about work for the next hour, about anything but Robert. Anthony seemed to be cautious when choosing his words, which was unlike him.

I ordered another round of drinks. This was going to be my fifth pint in the afternoon on an empty stomach. I was drunk.

"Are you sure you're ok?" Anthony asked again. I winked at him as I brushed off his comment,

THE DETERMINIST

We settled our tabs and parted ways. Not looking at my phone for the last two hours was smart, but getting this drunk was a problem. On the way home I detoured past the hockey rink and stood out in front of it for a moment. Contemplating whether or not to go in.

Deciding against it, I turned and walked home, not knowing what I was about to walk into. Would Robert be there, would Clayton?

I entered the house, only realizing how hot it was outside by the rush of cold air that hit me. The house was empty, Roberts hockey equipment was next to the door that led to the basement. He must have dropped it off in a hurry.

I walked into the kitchen and had a glass of water. Seeing my half-eaten sandwich and empty beer cans on the table I decided I needed to sleep off the effects of the beer.

Looking at my phone, I still had no text from Robert. I texted him that I had gotten home. Making my way to bed, I slumped, still in my clothes onto the pillow and fell straight asleep.

***

Waking up with a hangover in the early evening is strange. I turned over and called out down the stairs "ROB?" I yelled. No answer. The clock on the bedside table said 8.30 pm. Where was he?

I reached for my phone and dialled his number. He picked up after a few rings.

"Hey, what's up?" he said, sounding out of breath, this was not our regular greeting to each other. He was panting into the phone.

"Where are you, I have been worried all afternoon?" I said back to him.

"I'm just with the hockey boys," he said back, I heard someone in the background laughing.

"Oh I didn't know that you guys were going to be partying, did you win?" I asked.

"Yup," he said shortly, I could hear something in the background that I couldn't quite figure out what it was. Robert sounded strained like he was walking fast.

"Can I come to meet you guys?" I asked. Straining to listen in on the phone.

"Ugh," Robert grunted, I knew that grunting noise. My heart sank. "Well are you going to be nice to me or not?" he said after a pause.

I knew that grunting noise very specifically, he was having sex. While on the phone to me. My head flashed red in my eyes. I was sure of what I had just heard. I felt my blood pumping in my ears. I could now hear what must have been Clayton moaning.

"Well, why don't I just stay here and when you are done fucking Clayton, you can sleep on the couch you fucking asshole. You really took a call while you're doing that, you fucking piece of shit." I blurted out. Instantly regretting it.

Robert hung up the phone. I began to cry. I didn't talk to people that way. I was overcome with anger. I tried to call him again. It went to voicemail.

"Just give me a call please," I mumbled into the voicemail.

I text him. 'Please call me back, I didn't mean to lash out like that'

I fell back onto the bed and began to cry. Loud sobs. Wailing. Standing up from the bed, I started walking out of our bedroom, towards the stairs down to the kitchen. Taking one step at a time, feeling weak, my knees buckled underneath me. I surrendered, and sat on the staircase, crying. After a few moments, I pulled myself up and stumbled through the kitchen to reach the foyer. I sat, looking at the door. My phone was silent in my hand. I tried to call Robert again. It went to voicemail.

I put my phone down and sat on the couch staring at the front door. My mind was racing. My body was still.

My eyelids were becoming droopy. I had been waiting, staring at the door for close to two hours. It was almost midnight, Robert had not come home.

'Hold steady, hold steady,' I kept repeating in my head.

I don't know when I had fallen asleep but my phone woke me up. It was 7 am. I was hungover and hungry, I felt weak. I hadn't eaten anything since the half sandwich the day before and drank 5 beers. I was dehydrated and devastated.

Still no sign of Robert. His phone was now going straight to voicemail. I sent a text to Arthur White.
'Hey, Robert is MIA and I am worried about him. I need your help'.

Arthur did not respond.

I quickly showered, catching a glimpse of myself in the mirror. I hadn't taken time to look subjectively at myself in a while. I was even thinner, now that I hadn't eaten in a while. My skin was sallow. I looked sad.

Making my way down the stairs, making sure my bag contained what was needed for a day at work at Mavericks. I made one final call to Robert. No answer.

Arriving at Mavericks for work, I went through the motions, no one else was there, crying while doing a daily setup was a new experience. As staff started to trickle in, I would flatly tell them where they would be working in the restaurant, and returned to the back of the bar, staring at my phone. Trying to call Robert from the restaurant phone was as unsuccessful as using my own.

Suddenly at noon, I started feeling an overwhelming sense of panic. Retreating to the office, I picked up the phone and called the other manager, Raj, who was supposed to be relieving me in the afternoon. I very quickly explained that I had a family emergency and needed to leave. He told me he would be there in fifteen minutes.

Raj showed up forty-five minutes later. I was standing out the front waiting for him to show up, not wanting to leave the restaurant without a manager on duty. I saw Raj strolling around the corner, at that moment, I turned and went to my bike, passing him telling him that I had to leave right now.

The anxiety I was feeling was reaching a new depth. While cycling, I didn't even stop for red lights, just darted between traffic. Knowing in my head that something was happening. My body knew something was happening. Something bad was happening at my home.

I turned the corner onto my street. As I did, I saw Arthur's car pull out of the driveway. My heart was thumping in my chest. Putting my bike away in the garage, I took a moment to prepare myself for what was about to happen.

I was about to have a relationship-ending argument with Robert. He had done some terrible things to me, but I am not sure if this is something I could ever forgive him for. What was I going to say? What if he asked me for forgiveness? How will I tell him that the only way forward would be to go to couples therapy? How will I express how badly he has hurt me?

I took a deep breath and decided to start by telling him that I loved him, but what he has done is close to unforgivable.
I walked out of the garage, lowered my shoulders and took another deep breath in. I opened the door.

Walking into the house I took a moment to settle myself. I put down my bag, took off my shoes. I noticed the smell of the place. It smelt like he had just walked in. The house felt calm.

"ROBERT!" I called up the staircase.

No answer.

Walking up the staircase towards the kitchen I noticed first that his work bag was gone. Then the MacBook was gone. I went further up into the bedroom. He wasn't there. I opened his top drawer. He had cleared out his work shirts and taken all the cash from where we stored tip money before putting it in the bank or safe.

He had been and gone.

I walked back down to the kitchen. There was something on the floor. A piece of paper, maybe he'd dropped it out of a pile of stuff in his haste. I moved closer and recognized his handwriting. How had I missed this? There was my name, written in large font. I stood over it and focused, I didn't want to touch it, it felt like crime scene evidence. My breath was caught, how long ago had he written this?

Greg-
Want you to know that I'm ok.
But neither one of us is happy. I just can't continue living this way.
At some point we can sit down and discuss how to split things up
But I am not flexible on trying to fix what is clearly broken.
I am moving out, I need to move on with my life.
Please take care of yourself.
Rob.

I dropped to the floor.

Everything went black around me and my stomach started curling in. I was panting. I lay on the floor for a moment not being able to breathe properly. My torso muscles had all contracted in and it felt like my body was trying to pull itself apart from the inside out. There was a loud pounding noise in my ears. I finally gasped, took a deep breath in, my body started to un-tense. I sat up. My head was still pounding. I was next to the fridge. I reached in and grabbed a beer, not taking my eyes off the note on the floor.

I guzzled the beer and opened another. Getting up, I walked up to our bedroom and into the bathroom.

His toothbrush and electric razor were gone.

Reaching into the medicine cabinet, opening the large format bottle of Tylenol, I put the bottle to my mouth and poured in half the container of pills. Then taking a sip of the beer to wash them down, I burped two of them up. Spitting them into the sink. I put the bottle back to my mouth a second time and poured more pills into my mouth. I took a second to hold them there. Then taking a swig of beer, I swallowed the contents of my mouth.

I sat on the edge of the bathtub, like I had done many times before. And felt a sense of serene calmness. This was it. The moment I have chosen to die.

My beer was finished. After a few minutes, I walked down the stairs to get another one. I stumbled on the last step. Feeling a churning in my stomach, probably from all the beer and Tylenol. It had been roughly ten minutes since I had taken it all.

While reaching into the fridge to get another beer, I felt a pain in my stomach.

I made it to the sink in time to vomit up the pills. They started streaming out of me, covered in a thick mucus-looking substance. The force of the bile also made me soil myself. I could feel my legs trembling as I fell to the floor of the kitchen. There was still vomit coming out of me. I took a sip of the beer I was drinking to try and clear out my mouth.

My nose and mouth were burning. I had hot tears coming out of my eyes.

It appeared that my stomach rejected all the Tylenol as if saying 'not today.' My body was fighting against me. My body knew better than to listen to an impulse.

I started to cry again. What was I doing? Tylenol wouldn't do the job. If I was serious about this I would have to get something stronger. I opened up the cupboard under the sink and reached in for the drain cleaner. After a moment, I found the right bottle. It was empty. I cried harder.

I crawled up the stairs to the bathroom, getting into the tub, I turned the shower on, having the water hit me and my soiled clothes all at once.

My voice box was sore from crying. My eyes were puffy. I was sure that my body had rejected every last pill I had swallowed, but maybe kept enough of the drug to alleviate the headache I had felt. Towelling myself down, I stepped out of the shower and walked naked into the bedroom. Still crying. I dressed in comfortable clothes, walked down to the kitchen and began to clean up the mess I made on the floor. I wiped everything off the grey slate tiles with paper towels, the upchuck leaving a green tinge on the grouting. I collected myself, not wanting to empty the sink full of upchuck and dirty paper towels, and sat at the kitchen table with a beer, paper and pen.

I was midway into writing a goodbye note to Robert when my phone rang.
    Lunging towards it I picked it up and answered without looking at the screen.

"You just leave a fucking note on the floor? Get home Robert. This is cruel," I said down the receiver, starting to cry again.

"Mate, what's going on?" I heard Anthony's voice on the earpiece.

I should have checked the screen.

"Ah shit sorry, I gotta go," I said back.
"Mate, what is this, what the fuck is happening, talk to me," Anthony said.

I said nothing in return and started crying. I could hear that he was driving.

"I'm on my way over mate," Anthony said as he hung up the phone.

***

By the time Anthony arrived. I had gone to the store to buy cigarettes and was sitting in the back garden smoking and drinking another beer.

"What happened?" Anthony asked as he stepped into the garden, I could sense his reaction to seeing me.

"Yesterday, just before I saw you, I had basically caught Robert cheating on me red-handed. I guess I didn't know what to do, so I just pretended nothing had happened." I replied.

"Red-handed? What do you mean?" Anthony said.

"His computer is full of texts and stuff about him and his boyfriend, it's fucked. And last night when I called him he was having sex, I could hear moaning and stuff." I answered.

Anthony took a moment and lowered his head. I could tell he was angry.

"What happened this morning?" he asked again.

"Well, when I called him last night, it was horrible and then he just didn't come home. I left the house early for work, but I was useless there. I got another manager to cover for me and came home after two hours, and when I got back he had left a note on the kitchen floor telling me that he was leaving me." I said, starting to cry again.

Anthony got up and walked back inside. I could see him walking into the kitchen and my heart sank as I realized the notes I had started to write were still on the table. I followed up after a moment, he was standing at the table, looking over what I had written. I panicked and walked towards the table. He picked up the page before I could reach it. And held it away from me. He stared at me in the eye and put a hand on my chest.

"What the fuck is this!?" Anthony yelled. "What the fuck have you done!?" he continued.

"I just, its, more that I was thinking about it, and it was stupid really... I just thought if I was just going to write out what I should say to him if he called" I stammered out, pathetically attempting to lie.

Anthony's eyes narrowed as he looked at me in a moment of disgust.

"Bullshit, this looks like a fucking suicide note," Anthony said, the vein on his left temple bulging out, a glisten on the waterline of his eyes.

"It's not. I just…" I started to cry again and sat down on a chair. "I just don't understand why he is doing this to me. I have done nothing wrong." now crying with my whole body.

Anthony placed the paper back down on the table and rubbed his eyes. He walked to the sink and poured a glass of water. I heard a gasp when he must have seen what was in there, the up-chuck of the pills, the foamy, bile-soaked paper towels. He sat back down at the table with me as I continued to cry and passed me the water.

He put his hand on my shoulder and leaned in closer to me.

"Drink this, " he said, gesturing to the water. I lifted my head to see that he was looking very intensely into my eyes. "Mate, I promise you, your life is going to get so much better."

"I just want him to come home. Can you call him for me?" I responded, still choking on tears.

"No mate, I think we should get out of here. Let's go pack you a bag and you can come and stay with me for a while." Anthony said.

"NO!" I said bolting upright. "What if he comes back and I am not here?" I blurted out.

Anthony stood, walked to the living room and sat on a couch. I could hear his phone buzzing.

"Who are you texting?" I called out.
"Caroline," he responded.

I didn't want her to know just yet, what was he doing this for. I needed more time with Robert to figure out what was happening and how to tell the people around me.

"Please don't," I called out.

"Mate, she is your sister, she might know what to do, I am not going to contact Robert... do you even know where he is?" Anthony called out.

I walked into the living room, still holding my glass of water. I sat awkwardly on the couch opposite Anthony. I could feel the unease in my torso still. My body felt poised to rip itself apart again.

"I don't know where he is, but I would guess he is at Arthur's place. Where else would he go?" I responded.

Caroline didn't respond right away, Anthony had forgotten about the time difference now she was back in Australia.
"I guess she is sleeping. Look mate, I know this is going to be hard to hear, but he is not coming back, and you know it. There is no sense staying here, you will drive yourself mad if you do. I think you should go upstairs, grab a few things and come to my place for a few days." Anthony said in a calm voice.

"Ant, I don't want to, I don't want to be gone if he comes back, for a few reasons. One, what if he comes back to talk to me and I am not here? Two, what if he comes back and takes everything?

He has already locked up all our money in the safe. He is being erratic right now and I am honestly scared." I said.

"Do you have the combination for the safe?" Anthony asked.

"I could never remember it, I used it so little... oh fuck, my passport is in there," I said, realizing that indeed, my passport was probably locked in there. Would he have done this intentionally?

"Ok, well what do you think we should do?" Anthony said.

"I am just going to sit here and have a beer, and wait for something to happen, it's not like he will be like this forever," I replied.

A thought crossed my mind that maybe Robert would have had the same thought that I had. That attempting suicide was a good idea. I shuddered as I thought this and took a big gulp of the open beer on the coffee table. I had lost count of how many beers I had consumed now.

"Why is he doing this to me?" I said softly.

"I know I said it before, but, you need to hear me when I say, I promise that, in a year from now, your life will be so much better. You have been in so much pain in this relationship for so long. We can all see it. He hasn't treated you well and today is just another example of this." Anthony said.

I was taken aback by his words. I hadn't imagined what my life without Robert would look like. What my movements in the world would be like. I tried to think about what I was like when I was single, before I had met Robert.

"I'm going back to black jeans and black t-shirts. I used to be so powerful." I said, half slurring my words.

I lit another cigarette. Anthony went and got two more beers, and returned to the living room. He sat down and opened both, handing one to me.

"You are going to be ok mate. This is going to suck. But you are going to be ok. I think that you should consider packing a bag and coming over to my place though " Anthony tried again.

"I just won't. I am staying here. He will have to come back at some stage and I am going to be here when he does." I replied.

Anthony and I sat mainly in silence, drinking beer for a while. He was looking at his phone. I was lighting a cigarette every fifteen minutes or so, smoking half of it and putting it out. It was a disgusting habit that I had given up two years before. They were soothing me now in a way that I couldn't deny.

Anthony kept a steady flow of beer coming out of the fridge. Getting up whenever he sensed that I had finished another one. We were both starting to be a little drunk. I was starting to feel a bit more numb. It was relieving.

The sun had set. It was dusk. I could smell the neighbours firing up their barbeques. The smell wafted into the living room.

"Fuck I am starving, aren't you hungry?" Anthony said.

I hadn't eaten anything other than beer since the day before.

THE DETERMINIST

Anthony rose from the couch and put a hand out to me. Gesturing to get up.

"C'mon mate. Let's get out of the house," he said.

Getting off the couch, realizing how drunk I was. I saw myself in the reflection of the mirror in the foyer. I looked terrible. I didn't care. We put on shoes and made our way out of the house.

"I am coming back here tonight. This isn't a kidnapping," I said to Anthony as I drunkenly fumbled to lock the door.

"Jesus Christ! I know mate," he replied.

We walked around the corner of the street. It was a lovely Sunday evening, people were barbequing, having little front garden dinners, and I wanted none of it. I wanted to scowl at all of them, did they not know about the tragedy that I was enduring? We made our way to a pub around the corner and sat at the bar.

"Oh look, there is a beer special on, look at that" I mustered out, keeping my head and voice low.

"I don't think more beer is what you need right now mate," Anthony said in a low voice as the bartender came over.

"Hey guys, how are you tonight?" the bartender said in a jovial and fast tone.

I pointed to the menu indicating that I wanted the beer special. An extra-large pint of domestic beer.

"Ah, in for the Sunday deal! Good stuff! And can I start you on any appetizers?" the bartender cheerily continued.

"No mate, just one of those for him and some water, and I'll take the cheeseburger, I am starving," Anthony said, closing his menu and handing it to the smiley man.

The bartender looked a little offended by my lack of attention. He dutifully filled the giant beer glass and placed it in front of me. Catching my eye as he slid it towards me, he seemed to understand that I was going through something.

I took a sip from the beer, feeling so feeble I wanted to cry.

Anthony's cheeseburger arrived and he ate it like someone was going to take it away from him. It was gone in less than a minute. To this point, I hadn't thought about what it must feel like for him to have walked into all this. I felt bad.

After I had finished my beer, Anthony turned to me.

"I mean what I was saying. You need to trust me that in one year from now, your life is going to be so much better, and unfortunately, his life is going to get worse. Things like what has happened today are choices that he makes. It is a pattern of someone who is self-destructive. You, on the other hand, are going to soar," Anthony said. I grimaced at him, fighting back tears.

Anthony and I left the bar and started walking to my home. As we turned onto my street, his phone started to buzz. He looked at it and turned to me.

"Caroline is awake and freaking out that you haven't answered your phone. You gotta call her," he said to me.

We reached the front door. He put a hand on my shoulder as I walked into the foyer.

"Ok mate, I had a ton of meetings in the morning. I think Caroline is about to call you. Do you need anything before I go?" he said to me.

The thought of walking back into my home alone was a little frightening.

"Nah, I should be ok. I'll shoot you a text when I hear from Robert." I responded.

Anthony put his hand on my shoulder again.

"You're going to be ok mate," he said, turning on his heel and walking away.

I walked through the foyer and to the kitchen to fetch another beer. I found my phone on the couch, it was blinking with missed calls. Picking it up, I scrolled through everything. A call from my boss from Mavericks, along with a text that read 'you ok?' Five missed calls from Caroline. No missed calls or texts from Robert.

I sat on the couch and lay down. The thought of going to the bed we had both shared not 48 hours ago was unbearable. I was tired and drunk. Returning the call to Caroline was going to be hard.

Dialling her number, I started to feel the full crying start again. She answered after a few seconds.

"Greg, what happened?" She was worried but didn't sound surprised.

"Robert left me, he left a note on the kitchen floor telling me he doesn't want me anymore and he is gone now," I said, starting to hysterically cry.

"Where has he gone?" she asked.

"I don't know, he is just gone," I replied.

Caroline was silent as I cried. She stayed on the line listening to me cry for around ten minutes.
"You are so loved. You are so loved, I got you. Do you need me to come over there?" she finally said when my crying had subsided.

"I don't know, probably not, I mean it would take a good week for you to get here from Melbourne, I just don't know. I gotta go to bed. I am so tired and drunk." I replied.

"Ok, but I just want you to know you are very loved if you need me to book you a flight to come home--" Caroline said
"He locked my passport in the safe" I interrupted her.

"Oh fuck, Greg, look this is going to be a difficult few days, I think you need to get some sleep and call me when you wake up, ok?" she said.

"ok, " I gulped between tears.

We said goodbye again. I clicked off the phone. Putting my head down on the pillow I dialled Robert's number again. It went straight to voicemail. I listened to his voice on the message. It was from a time when he sounded happy. I hung up before it was time for me to speak to the message bank.

Rolling into the couch again, I started to fall asleep. Passing out on the couch. Finally not crying.

CHAPTER 11

Waking up the way you feel every morning, warm, comfortable. There was a small patch of dryness in my mouth from sleeping with my mouth open. Opening my eyes, looking out over the living room, my body felt momentarily numb, my limbs loose. My stomach was twisting and making noises as I woke. I felt alert and startled suddenly.

The severity of what had happened the day before washed through me. I felt it affecting every part of my body that had been calm and still only a few moments ago. My fingers clenched. My torso tensed. My toes curled, and my head started pounding. I let out a small sob.

I reached for my phone. Clicking the screen on, there wasn't much battery left, I would have to eventually face the task of walking into the bedroom to retrieve the charging cable. The time was 7.44 am. Robert had left me. I was alone.

I rose from the couch, more tears coming from my eyes. I reached for the half-drunk beer on the coffee table from the day before and finished it in one gulp. I looked at the table in front of me and at the floor. Cigarette ash was spotting on the table. A weathered empty beer can had a burnt-out cigarette butt protruding from it.

This is my bleakest moment. My phone blinked at me. Caroline had messaged.

7:18 am 'Just on my way to work. Hope you take care of yourself today. Love you.'

I couldn't bring myself to answer her. Laying on the couch staring at the ceiling, I wondered what Robert would be doing. 'What is he doing?' asking myself out loud.

Sitting bolt upright. I knew what he would be doing. He would be going to work. His bus would be stopping past the hotel two blocks from our home to pick up tourists within the next hour. I jumped away from the couch.

Venturing into the bedroom to plug in my phone, trying not to look at his things casually placed around the room, I change into street clothes. I haven't eaten in two days now. My clothes are loose.

Making my way down to the foyer of the house, placing a ball cap on to hide my hair, I took another breath as I closed the front door behind me. I headed in the direction of the hotel, there was an apartment building across the street from it with a view of where his bus would pull up, if, *if* he was working.

I sat down on the bench outside the building staring at the hotel. I lit a cigarette. Checking my watch, it was now 8.25 am.
Any moment now. My cigarette burnt out.

I looked down the street as a large white coach bus turned the corner. I could tell Robert was in the driver's seat. My heart twisted in my chest, my stomach jumped and I could hear the blood in my ears thumping in time with my heart.

I watched as he descended from the bus and started talking to the tourists.

"Look up at me buddy," I whispered to myself, longing just to see his face.

He ushered everyone onto the coach and stood in front of it checking his radio and phone. His eyes turned to meet mine. I stared at him. The 30 meters of traffic between us disappeared. We were locked in eye contact. He looked at me and his eyes dropped. The corners of his mouth drooped. His face turned grey. As he saw me his chin raised up and his whole head followed. He turned and spun into his shoulder. Cars passed, obscuring my view of him. He was back behind the front of the coach bus before I could register what was happening.

The idling coach roared to life. The exhaust pushed out a small puff of soot. I was staring at him in the driver's seat. His eyes were fixed forwards. He moved determinedly into the open lane and drove his bus full of tourists away.

Slumping down on the bench, I began to cry. I wanted to be at home on my couch and out of the sun, away from the traffic. Pulling myself up, I started back to the house, holding my sides as I walked.

Coming through the front door was silent. Calm, unnerving calm. I took off my shoes and went to the kitchen. I pulled three beers out of the fridge and retreated to the living room. Turning on the TV and rolling into the nook of the couch I had slept in.

***

It was afternoon. I had rotated between daytime TV and the opening scenes of a slew of bad romance movies on Netflix, unable to focus on any of them for long. I had finished the packet of cigarettes and had stocked the fridge with more beer from the basement.

I walked out into the street and towards the corner store. I needed more cigarettes. I felt light, feeble. Like I could be blown over by a gust of wind. Reaching the corner store, opening the door, the cashier stared at me.

"Belmont 25, kings, please," I muttered to the cashier.
He reached behind him and put them on the counter. He stared at me.

"Card or cash?" he said.

"Credit card," I said, letting out a large gulp that slowly turned into a shuddering sob.

I waved my card over the receiver and retrieved the packet of cigarettes. Turning sharply out of the gaze of the cashier I made my way to the door, desperate to disengage with the outside world and it's humanity.

"AYE MAN!" the cashier yelled out to me. "YOU LEFT YOUR WALLET HERE" he continued to yell.

I turned, now sobbing and made my way back to the register to retrieve my wallet.

I had never felt this pathetic.

Arriving home from the store, I went back upstairs to check my charging phone. There were no missed calls. No new texts. I took the phone, its battery replenished, with me back down to the living room, lit another cigarette and sat. I was watching Sex and the City, the movie. Arguably the worst movie in the last ten years.

I had replayed the part when Carrie stops her limo, jumps out in traffic and throws her bouquet at Mr. Big about eight times, nearly jamming the button on the remote. I was watching it with satisfaction. The pain in Sarah Jessica Parker's face was satisfying. The confusion in Chris Noth's face was infuriating. He knew he had done wrong.

I lit another cigarette.

***

I must have fallen asleep at some point, my phone was buzzing at me. It was Caroline.

"Hi," I said breathlessly to her.
"How are you doing?" she replied.

"I don't know," I said.
"Did you eat today?" Caroline probed.

"Why did we watch stupid romance movies when we were kids? It sets us up to fail." I interrupted her line of questioning.
"Are you ok?" Caroline said.

THE DETERMINIST

"No. I think I need to sleep." I said softly.

***

5 am in the summer in Toronto is normally a lovely time. It is humid, though not overwhelmingly so. It is warm, but still a little chilly from the early morning. The city smells clean. Toronto is a late start city. 5 am is a very calm time.

I sat in the back garden smoking a cigarette, sipping the last of a beer that I woke up next to. I needed to eat.

At 7 am the supermarket would be open.

I ascended the stairs to the bedroom and looked on the floor for my street shorts. I fetched a fresh pair of underwear and socks from a drawer, fondled through the wardrobe for a shirt, and walked into the bathroom.
Turning on the shower I felt light, untouchable. The water didn't even have much effect on my skin. I didn't bother with soap. Just stood in the shower. I had no tears left to cry. I was numb.

I dressed myself, taking care to look in the mirror and make sure I didn't look too sad.

Leaving the house, I walked promptly across the street towards the supermarket. It was 6.55 am.

I was a few moments early. The doors were open to the store anyway. I let myself in, picked up a basket and walked to the 'ready to eat' section. Without looking at prices or dates, I scooped up two packets of sushi. I made my way to the fruit section and selected some bananas. I wandered to the bakery aisle. The good quality bread that I normally favoured was of no interest. I picked up a loaf of bread from the ready-pack section.

I went through the checkout wordlessly.

Walking home, I felt like my legs were blocks of cement. My torso was still holding the tension from the panic of being in public. Everything in my body was tense and on alert. I felt like a wild animal.

"Greg! Sweet man! I thought that was you" I heard someone say from behind me.

I turned around. It was Graham. A friend of Roberts who was lovely and kind. I stared at him and started shaking my head. He looked at me

"Are, are you ok?" Graham said. His face went from his usual smile to a grimace of concern.

"FUCK OFF," I said forcibly to him, turning on my heels to walk away.

I felt horrible. Graham was nice enough. He would have no issue helping me if I needed it. I felt bad for lashing out at an unsuspecting acquaintance but continued walking towards home. Graham would hear about what had happened and forgive me later.

Passing over the threshold, and into the foyer, I took my pants and shirt off. The day was already starting to get hot.

THE DETERMINIST

I sat in the living room and pulled out my supermarket haul.

Opening the sushi, I contemplated it for a moment. I didn't want to eat. I knew I should.

I took one of the pieces into my fingers. I looked at it for another moment. I shoved it into my mouth. Chewing for a half moment, I tried to swallow. The dry rice and seaweed were stuck in my throat. I reached for a beer. Every can on the table was empty or had a cigarette butt coming out of it.

Choking, I walked up to the kitchen. Yanking open the fridge, I reached for a can of beer, and in one swift motion, opened it while raising it to my lips. I took a painful gulp as I felt every grain of rice pass my chapped esophagus. The burning feeling from vomiting days before was returning. It was strangely satisfying. My body was responding physically to its emotional state, like we were on the same team. strangely validating.

I returned to the couch, clicking on the TV to make some noise, I set about finishing the small offering of sushi I had procured. Struggling through every piece. The bread would have to wait. Every morsel of food felt like a razor blade working its way down my dry, swollen throat.

I leaned back on the couch and swung my legs up. I was half sitting, half lounging. My phone buzzed, I felt drowsy. My eyes became heavy as I fell asleep.

***

The buzzing of my phone was the first thing that I had noticed. I hadn't opened my eyes yet.

I reached for the phone. I answered the call as I brought it to my ear.

"Just checking that you didn't forget you have therapy tonight mate," Anthony said. I could hear the clatter of the restaurant he worked in behind his words.

"I know," I replied.

"Just be honest with her and tell her everything, you pay for her. And make sure you take a shower beforehand." Anthony continued. There was a silence in him, I could tell that he had pulled the receiver away from his mouth for a moment to talk to someone else. "Just make sure you get there, I'll call you tonight," he obviously needed to get off the phone.

"Ok," I replied flatly.

The phone clicked off. I could taste beer and rice from before lingering in my mouth. I had been asleep for 4 hours.

I emailed my therapist.
'It happened, Robert left me, I will see you tonight at 6'

***

The Uber driver was perfectly quiet on the journey to the therapist's office.

I stood out the front of her building for a few minutes, smoking a cigarette before walking to the door. I pressed the doorbell and heard the muffled tone. The door opened. She cocked her head to the side.

"Ok, this is ok, let's go," she said. She gave me a quick glance up and down.

I wondered if she had ever had to deal with a patient that was actively having his life destroyed by a relationship. I followed her into her session room and sat down. I looked around not wanting to lock eyes with her.
"Gregory, you are going to be ok." she started.

"I did nothing wrong," I whispered.

"I know, it might be helpful if we concentrate on some-" she was saying slowly, I cut her off.

"I did nothing wrong. I followed every rule that I was supposed to. I kept myself nice, I kept myself docile. I made myself everything that he would want. And still, this didn't work. I came to you for help." My voice was still quiet, though cutting.

"Yes, Gregory but you need to remember-" she started again.

"I came to you for help and you gave me the reasons why this might not work. You set me up for failure. How many failed marriages are you responsible for?" I said, feeling hot tears come down from my face, my voice getting a little louder.

She remained unblinking and silent. Staring at me.

"Why didn't you just tell me to go on a fucking diet and sort my shit out. Why didn't you just prescribe me some fucking antidepressants and send me on my fucking way, MY LIFE IS RUINED RIGHT NOW, ROBERT IS GONE AND HE ISN'T COMING BACK. YOU

FUCKED UP!" I screamed, unaware of the fact that I was now standing.

I sat back down, panting and ashamed of what I had said. Why did I just say that?

"Gregory, I understand that you are going through possibly one of the hardest moments of your life right now," she took a breath in "But I need you to remain calm and remember that this is my office." she continued. Her demeanour turned from calm to stern. "I don't appreciate being yelled at. I am here to help you, and I want nothing more than to help you navigate through this. But getting upset with me is not going to move any outcome in either direction." she finished.

I sat back in the chair. I felt the pull of my torso again. The feeling like it was going to rip me apart from the inside.

"I just hate this," I muttered, my body contracting on itself again. Pulling my face down towards my knees as I sat.

Sitting weeping, I was too ashamed to look up.

"The hardest part of separation is learning how to do things again by yourself," she said softly. "Your brain is wired to remember the actions of the closest person around you. To accommodate their daily rituals, and for your rituals to rely on theirs. Your brain will have to unlearn that." she concluded. Reaching towards me, she offered a box of tissues. Her regular notepad was on the floor.

"You will learn how to be the person you can be without him. And it will be hard." she paused as I made a sudden move for the box of tissues. "You were happy before you met him. And yes, you had an amazing time being in love with him. But you will move past this." How did she sound so calm? Had she rehearsed this? Had she known this was coming?

Why was everyone convinced of moving me past what had happened when I hadn't even talked to Robert.

"It's too hard… and I did nothing wrong." I whimpered. My voice was pure despair.

"All you could do is be the person you are. Loving and caring for him," she said slowly, matching the rhythm of my speech. "Gregory, you may not want to hear this, but I need you to look at me."

I sniffled for another minute, wondering what could she possibly have to offer me right now that could help.

"What?" I asked.

"One theme I have noticed from the last eighteen months is, you have never spoken a nice word about Robert," her eyes gaged me as she spoke each word carefully.

I remained silent and weeping, suddenly unable to look away from her. Was it true? Had I never said a good thing about Robert? I had talked to her about a lot of things in my relationship with him but was never ready to talk about the cheating. I hadn't even told her about the other guys.

"He has been having an affair for the last few months with a nineteen-year-old Brazilian guy named Clayton. I looked him up on Facebook. He is here studying," the words fell out of me. I wasn't sure I had made them complete in my head before they rolled out of my mouth.

"Ok, tell me about what you know," she said, picking up her notepad from the floor next to her chair, nestling back into her role as a therapist.

"I looked him up on Facebook a few months ago when I realized what was happening. I saw his name pop up on the laptop's iChat a few times. He was sending all kinds of messages to Robert, I cannot tell if Robert was leading him on or if it was genuine," I said. "He seems to know about me, and Robert is painting a picture of me being a horrible partner. Like I am some sort of villain" I concluded.

"Did you confront Robert about this?" she asked.

"No, but on Friday night, he knew I saw a text from this guy. It was tense between us. And on Saturday I caught him lying to me to not come to his hockey game, so he could bring this other guy," I continued.

"What did you do?" she probed.

"I went for a few beers with Anthony and didn't say anything about it. I guess I was in a bit of shock from it all. When it was late and he still wasn't home on Saturday night, I called him," I dropped my head, realizing that reliving this moment will never get any easier. "I am pretty sure that when he answered the phone he was having sex with this other guy, as he was talking to me." I shuddered and started shaking my head.

"Gregory that is awful, that is truly awful. Do you need to take a break?" she said calmly.

"No, I don't," I replied, fetching another tissue from the box on the table. "When I realized what was happening, I went mad. I yelled down the phone at him. I became everything that he told me I was. But it was just so mean of him to do that to me," my body now wracked with sobbing, shoulders shuddering, tears running down my face.

"You don't need to relive this moment now," she said. "What you can do is concentrate on how to stop the bleeding of the situation. What are some steps you can take to fortify yourself against this? Maybe consider your living situation moving forward… Separation of assets…" she trailed off.

"I haven't even spoken to him, who knows where he is? Do you know? You could call Arthur White and ask him. He is your colleague. He will know." I said, noting a flash of retraction in her face as I said it. Was she mistaking my desperation for hostility?

"Greg, you need to concentrate on yourself for now. You need to ask for help from some of the people around you. Is there someone you can call, or stay with?" she asked.

Remaining silent for a moment after she had said this, her eyes searched over me. I could feel her eyes surveying every shudder, evaluating each movement, cautiously studying every part of me.

"I'm not going to kill myself," I said, sensing that was what she needed to know.

"I need to know that you are safe and comfortable before you leave this office. We do have a few moments left in the session, why don't we spend them putting together a plan of who to call when you are feeling low. You know you can always contact me, just send an email and I will schedule a time," she said. Her eyes searching me again.

"I know, I have people. Anthony has been great. I have been texting with Caroline. I think I just want to go to sleep for most of the time though," I concluded.

Our session ended. We rose, I was unsteady again on my feet and made my way down the hall of her office towards the door. Reaching the street I started walking towards the closest intersection.

I stood outside a bar waiting for my Uber and peered through the windows. There was a live band playing and people were sitting listening. I contemplated going inside to join them. I was still dressed in loose-fitting shorts and a tee-shirt, I could pass as a casual patron, a lover of live music, enjoying a beer and some solitude on this summer evening. Then my eyes welled up again. Would I ever be able to sit and enjoy music again?

My Uber arrived, I slumped in the back seat, determined to stay silent. A short trip back to the safety of my couch, an overflowing ashtray and a fridge full of alcohol.

Arriving back at home, I fetched two cans of beer from the fridge and sat down on the couch, clicked on the TV, and scrolled through the channels to find something sombre to watch. I was suddenly very tired. That short outing had been taxing and felt longer than it was.

THE DETERMINIST

Leaning into the crook of the couch I had been sleeping in, nestling myself in, falling asleep within a few moments.

CHAPTER 12

"Hey bud," Robert was standing over me. "Buddy, wake up."

I could tell that I was dreaming. Feeling the uncertainness of his presence, I didn't want to open my eyes. I felt a wisp of hope run through me, could this be real? Was he standing over me as I dreamed of him?

Opening my eyes, already crying as I roused. Robert was not there. There was a strange feeling in my arms, I had been sleeping on them for a while. Guessing that today would be spent much like the last two days, there was no need to move from this position right now. Laying on this couch in the way I was, twisted against myself, a slow stream of tears falling from my eyes.

Crying seemed to help, at this point, it was soft whimpers and sobs. Having panic attacks during the last few days after leaving therapy had left my torso rigid most of the time. There was a stiffness to me. A woodenness.

Staring at the ceiling as I cried I looked at my phone, it blinked at me. Caroline was checking in with me at least every six hours, I had probably slept through one of her calls. But when I clicked the screen on, I was jolted out of the reverie. There was a missed call from Robert. I had slept through a call, the time stamp on it was 25 minutes ago.

Why was I asleep during this? I had a chance to hear him talk to me but I was asleep like an idiot. 'You stupid fucking idiot' I mumbled to myself.

Deciding to check the voicemail before calling him back, I clicked through to the message.

'Hey, we need to have a talk. Let's organize a time to meet….ah yeah… Bye," Robert's voice sounded shaky and tired. It also sounded like he was reading from a script. Maybe he was.

Dialling his number, I cleared my throat and took a sip of water from a glass that was nestled amongst the empty beer cans on the coffee table. As the tone rang, my phone buzzed twice with incoming text messages. I looked quickly at my phone, it was from Robert. I hung up to read the texts.

'Can't talk right now, busy.' the first one read.
'Want to meet to discuss things.' the second text read.

'Yes, I can meet tomorrow, at the house?' I responded.

Staring at my phone expecting a response, I started to feel something inside me turn, I was starving, my stomach grumbled loudly. Walking up the stairs to the kitchen I reached into the fridge for some bread. A sandwich would be kind on my empty stomach.

Munching gingerly through the bread and vegemite I clicked my phone back on. Still no response. What was taking him so long to respond? He was probably working.

I wondered how he could just carry on as normal with his life after destroying everything in mine.

My fingers lingered on the sandwich on the plate, I couldn't take another bite. I didn't want to throw it out either. I looked around the kitchen.

Empty beer cans and water glasses. Some packets of various snacks that had been opened and abandoned after a bite.

I started cleaning up. Loading the glasses into the dishwasher. I stopped as I turned on the tap, thinking about all the times I had prepared a meal for Robert in this kitchen. How just a few weeks earlier I'd hosted a gathering of friends and family for his birthday. How grateful he was that I made a great party for him. How he had held me so close and kissed me that night telling me that it was one of the best nights he had ever had.

I then remembered that he had not come home until very late the next night. How he told me he was working, and remembering how I knew in my gut that he was with someone else. Celebrating his birthday in his own way.

Crying, I abandoned the kitchen, taking with me the now-standard three cans of beer to the couch. My phone buzzed. It was Robert.

'Let's meet tomorrow at Allen Gardens at 10 am.' Robert texted.

THE DETERMINIST

I felt a moment of relief. He was going to meet me. I sat back on the couch and started thinking about the things I wanted to say to him. I wanted to tell him it was ok and to come home. I wanted to hit him with a baseball bat.

***

"Well, what are you going to say to him?" asked Anthony over the phone.

"I think I am going to just wait and see what comes naturally, I mean what if I see him and he is begging me to come home, what if he wants to move back, what if, you know..?" I responded.

"I think you should prepare yourself for him to tell you what he wrote in that letter. But I think you should also prepare yourself to feel ok with it. He is not coming home" Anthony said.

I paused to take in what Anthony had said to me.

"What if he is drawing me out of the house so he can come in and take more of our stuff, or lock me out?" I said. That thought had been lingering somewhere in the depths of my mind since the park meeting was arranged.

"Do you really think he would do that?" Anthony asked.

"I mean, he has done worse things to me. I think that he might be trying to pull me out of the house so he can change the locks." I continued.

"You sound paranoid, when did you last sleep?" Anthony asked.

It was a little far-fetched, but not out of the realm of what could happen. He had done worse things to me.

I drifted down to the garden with a beer and a cigarette. It had been another hot day in the city. It was just starting to cool off as people were turning on their barbecues, settling in for another cruisey summer night. Sitting on the patio furniture, I started thinking about what Anthony had said. Was it paranoid of me to think that Robert would change the locks while I was out? I never thought he'd end our seven-year relationship with a fucking note on the kitchen floor. I figured I should be prepared for more ruthless cruelty.

From my chair in the garden, I heard my neighbour turning on his barbeque. Through the gap in the fence, I saw a kind eye peeping through. Why can I not remember this man's name? I had spoken to him a few times. I had heard his laugh over the fence during the summer.

"Hey Greg, I heard some commotion through the wall over the last few days," he said.

"I'm sorry, Robert left me," I replied. No anesthesia for the friendly neighbour, the words came out robotically, what was the point in sugarcoating anything?

I assumed I'd shocked him when he lowered his eye and moved away from the gap, but then his whole face appeared as he climbed up and leaned over the top of the fence.

"Are you ok?" He asked gently.

THE DETERMINIST

I moved in my seat to put out my cigarette. A beer can was now starting to overflow with soggy cigarette butts. I leaned forward to stub out my cigarette, adding to the overflow of the designated beer can turned ashtray, and decided not to answer him. I got up from my seat and walked back inside. Shutting the door I looked back to see him lowering off the fence and back into his garden, his barbeque awaiting. I felt ashamed of my anti-social behaviour, but also knew that the friendly neighbour would understand.

Retreating into the couch, I fell asleep after a few hours of mindless TV, beers and a few more cigarettes.

***

It is 9:30 am. Standing looking at my reflection, anxiety started to inch its way up my back. I was wearing skinny jeans and a tank top. I looked ok, considering. I put my hair into a backwards ballcap. On the way downstairs I set up my iPad with the camera facing the front door and pressed record. I had decided early that morning that if I captured someone coming into the house when I was gone, then my paranoia was valid.

Making my way out the door and down the street, I felt slightly lighter, and excited. I was going to see him. I was going to see my partner and figure all of this out. Or he was baiting me to the park so he could ransack the house.

I stood at the corner of the park waiting for Robert. Ten minutes passed, I sat on a bench and looked at my phone.

I looked up the street and saw him. He looked grey and was wearing shorts and a stained sweater. He had sunglasses on. He raised a hand to wave at me and crossed the road.

Tears started collecting in the corners of my eyes.

He pulled me into a hug and tried to kiss me on the face. I had my hands barred up against his chest and was pushing him away. I could feel him draw me in closer. His arms had always been strong. I very quickly became angry and wanted to push him away. I couldn't talk. I had my head in his chest. He pulled me in closer. He held me as I cried. Tightly. I felt like I was allergic to him.

Suddenly I felt a shift in the way he held me. He was moving the way he was holding me and his hips shifted towards me. He started pressing himself into me with purpose. He had an erection. It was pressing into my stomach. He was taller than me by a foot and it is how our bodies lined up. He took me by the wrist and pushed my hand toward his groin. He was trying to lead my hand to his erection. I was shocked. We were standing outside a dog park.

I freed myself from his grip and watched as he moved to conceal himself, his head hanging low as he started to sob. I took him by the hand and led him into the park, to a more secluded area, away from the hubbub of the dog park.

We sat at a bench, close to each other. I could see the look of shame on his face.

"Why did you do that?" I asked.

"I just, I don't really know, I was…" Robert trailed off and stopped talking.

"You've just made this even more confusing," I said.

"I just can't, I wasn't built to be in relationships. I just find it hard," Robert said.

"I think you are confusing this, I think you wanted to hurt me, and you did, but now you're turned on by it. What the actual fuck?" I said softly after a few moments.

Robert looked at me and started to cry, "I didn't want to hurt you" he whimpered.

"Then why did you do it like this?" I asked.

Robert took a few moments of silence.

"Where are you staying?" I asked.

"I am around, but I don't want to tell you," he said.

"What do you think I am going to do? Your parents called me and I had to tell them I didn't know where you were…" I said. Robert raised his head and looked at me sharply.
"What did you tell them?" he asked quickly.

"I didn't tell them about your boyfriends," I said back to him.

"See, that is why this won't work. Comments like that. Why are you so mean?" Robert asked me with childlike confusion.

"How am I the one to blame for this? I have done literally nothing wrong. I have been trying so hard for so long Rob. You have been fucking this up, and now you have fucked it up more." I said quietly, it poured out of me uncontrollably.

I was bewildering myself. Before he arrived I thought I wanted to fix this, but seeing him made me suddenly mad. All of the heartbreak from the last few days was coming out in aggression. I needed to keep myself calm.

"Look, I am just trying to stop the bleeding on this Rob. I need to stop the bleeding in my life. I am working way too much. And whatever we have become, you don't want anymore. You have made that pretty clear," I said, moving away from him and angling my body on the bench. I was surprising myself with each word. Did I really want this? Did my brain know better than my heart? Or was my gut speaking? Whatever it was, it felt right. I stayed calm... "Now, we have some logistics to figure out." I finished.

"What are you talking about?" Robert looked at me.

"Like I said... You've made it very clear what you want. I have the note to prove it. It's going to be painful, and time will tell if it's a mistake or not. But you want to leave, so I need to figure out how this will work. Kind of like our whole relationship dynamic, now that I think back. You've made a decision without talking to me about it, and I'll work to ensure this happens in a way that is fair for us both," I said, quietly amazed at my diplomacy.

"See, you are so fucking mean, why are you treating me like this?" Robert said.

THE DETERMINIST

I sat back, bewildered once more. He reached out a hand and pulled me towards him. His large and muscular body made short work of shuffling me along the bench. He started crying again. I put my hand on his knee. I had stopped crying. Watching him like this, rose-coloured glasses smashed on the ground, allowed me to see how he had actually manipulated our entire relationship to ensure that his desires were my priority, and mine were never considered. My role was to keep him happy.

"We gotta start telling each other what we want," I said softly.

"I don't know," Robert said and started sobbing again.

I put my hand on his back and started to rub his shoulders. Watching him shift in his seat again. He looked me in the eyes.

"I love you and that's why this is so hard," he said

"What is so hard?" I asked.

"I can't be in a relationship with you anymore but I love you and I don't know what decision is the right one to make," Robert said.

"This is going to be hard on both of us. I think maybe we should try and help each other out with this." I said.

"What does that mean?" Robert said, looking at me with an anxious look on his face

"It means that we are going to do fairly by each other. I think that we should do this in a way that is respectful, that honours what we had, and gives it the ending we each deserve," I said.

Robert looked relieved.

We rose off the bench and started walking towards the edge of the park.

"Walk me back to the house?" I asked, looking up at him. The moment I did, he looked at me, put his hand on my face and leaned down to kiss me. It felt like everything it has always been, it felt safe and loving and fine. I started to cry again.

We crossed the street and walked down towards the house. He reached down and grabbed my hand and held it.

"We are going to be ok, right?" he asked me.

"What do you mean? You want to come home right now?" I asked.

Robert took a moment.

"I don't know what I mean. But I do know that our relationship is over, I am going to walk you home but that is it," Robert said.

I choked up. I felt myself starting to cry again. We were close to the house, I just needed to get there and then I could cry all I wanted. Robert held my hand tightly.

We arrived at the door and Robert pulled me into a hug. I felt him starting to pull away and I held onto him closer. I was so angry at him but also wanted him to come inside so we could forget about everything that had happened in the last month. We could console ourselves together as we had done before.

I started to cry harder.

"Don't leave me here alone," I pleaded with him.

I felt him pull away. He was looking away from me. I tried to get him to look me in the eyes. He wouldn't.

"No," he replied.

He put his hands on my shoulders and pushed me to the side, as I turned he let go of me and my legs gave out. I fell down at the door and started crying. He stopped for a minute but not turning around, and then kept walking. I watched through my tears as he made his way up the street. Away from me.

I sat slumped in the front doorway of the house we once shared.
I pulled myself up slowly and staggered towards the door. Passing the threshold and walking into the house. It was quiet. Strangely peaceful.

PART 3

CHAPTER 13

Joseph looked down at his phone, toggling the pages on the screen to locate the running tracker app. His finger hovered above the record button.

"Ready?" he asked me. I nodded, adjusting my headband.

We started out along the footpath towards Bloor Street, turning right and following across the Prince Edward Viaduct. It was lit up with orange and blue lights. As Joseph would step in front of me to run past pedestrians, I could see steam rising from his back. He was pushing forward at a faster pace than he normally had. We turned right onto Broadview and made our way down towards Riverdale Park. I reached out and tapped his shoulder.

"Do you want to do the big staircase? Or go down to the Dundas bridge?" I asked, panting between each word. Hoping he would say the bridge.

"Let's do the stairs, I feel like a challenge," he replied.

THE DETERMINIST

We took a steep turn down to the river bank and continued towards the long and steep staircase on the west side of Riverdale Park.

I have always had to be in the right mood to run up those stairs. Ten years of running in this park and I only force myself to do it when absolutely necessary. They are long and unrelenting, it feels like people stop just to watch you attempt the climb. I bounded up in front of Joseph, taking the stairs two at a time. I slowed down towards the top, purposefully making myself look fatigued. He caught up to me. We started to bound up the last few steps together. I stifled a giggle as I purposefully slammed my foot down on the top step.

"I won!" I declared.

Joseph looked up at me as I jumped onto a bench, grinning with my hands in the air, revelling in the small victory.

We looked out over the view to the east of the city. There were a fair few people out in the park. The weather had finally started to shift from February's winter to March's spring, and unseasonably early. Given we had spent the winter in lockdown trying to lower the case numbers from the pandemic it was nice to see people out, albeit clustered in small groups together and wearing masks.

We took a moment on the top of the stairs to catch our breath and enjoy the view from the top. Eventually, I took him by the hand and pulled him in the direction of the running route I had planned in my head.

With a groan he followed, and we paced through the park towards Cabbagetown. We turned the corner onto Allen Gardens. I passed the bench I had sat on with Robert 18 months ago. I stopped running, I had passed this bench many other times, but today felt different. Joseph slowed down in front of me, turning to see me approaching the bench.

"Oh thank god, I know that we are close to home but I am cooked," Joseph said with a sigh.

He reached for his phone and pressed stop on the running app on his phone. Our run was over. I could see my breath in the air. Sitting down on the bench, Joseph walked over and put his hands on my shoulders.

"You ok babe?" he asked. His glasses had fogged up.
I lingered on my response. I want to tell him this is an important space for me, how revealing should I be?

"Yeah, I am. I don't know what I did to deserve you," I said sweetly to him.

He giggled. "Gross," he muttered as he leaned in to kiss me.

We made our way back to my apartment, peeling our sweaty running clothes off as we passed through the door. Walking into the kitchen to drink water, we both looked at each other. My skin was flushed red. He was still sweating. We sat down on yoga mats like we tended to do after our runs.

I could feel the need to tell him something. If there was a limit to what you tell your boyfriend about yourself, I had surely hit that boundary months ago and was now on borrowed time.

Joseph would listen, without judgment. He was kind and compassionate. He understood that I had a past that involved some people doing some bad things to me. In the beginning, it affected how I acted around him, until one day I just decided to tell him everything. I figured he would either catch on to me being cagey and not telling him when something was wrong and lose interest in me, or I could be honest. If he was still uninterested at least I would know it was for me as a person, not who I created to mask parts of my past with.

"I just got reminded of something when we finished our run today. That bench we passed that I sat down on. It was somewhere I used to spend a lot of time." I continued. "It was where a weird conversation with my ex happened, and for a few months afterwards I would sit there for hours. One day I even fell asleep on it. I just kinda used it as a sulking spot. Like the scene of the crime. I just remember how sad I once was." I finished.

"Yeah, but you don't do that anymore babe, do you?" Joseph replied.

"God no!" I exhaled into the stretch.

"Right, you're better and yeah there is stuff in the past but you are moved on with it all." he calmly concluded, with a matter-of-fact look on his face. He was right, I had moved on.

We went about our stretches, I turned on the news, Ontario was in its third wave of the pandemic. The vaccination program had started, but there were distribution issues which meant it was going to be a longer wait to get the needles into our arms. We were coming up on a year of lockdowns. Every other first-world country seemed to be progressing, or at least moving past the lockdown stage. Ontario was still seeing 3500 positive cases a day. People were still dying in alarming numbers. It distressed me, but I wanted to know what was happening.

"Turn that off babe, let's just take the night off from the news," Joseph said.

I didn't have any objection. Despite needing to stay informed, I had started regulating my intake of news to preserve my mental health. We sat looking outside my window for a moment. Joseph rose from the yoga mat and smiled at me.

"Ok babe, I've got to go home and get ready for work tomorrow," Joseph sighed.

We moved towards the front door. He leaned in and kissed me as he put his coat and mask on. He had stopped sweating and still had a post-run glow, the type you can only get from running in the cold.

"Bye, love you," Joseph winked at me.

I pulled down his mask and kissed him. "I love you too," I said.

He smiled at me and pulled his mask back up as he opened the door and left. I closed the door behind him, then walked into the living room. Sitting against the wall on my yoga mat, I stared out the window thinking. I had spent hours and hours sitting at that park bench after Robert had done what he'd done. All the time I spent in that part of the park, thinking about what had happened. There was probably still a mark where I used to butt out cigarettes, a habit I had now kicked. I left a huge part of myself on that bench.

My phone buzzed, a reminder about the appointment I had that night. A therapy session. I had gone down to once every two weeks for therapy. During lockdown there was not too much happening, work was easy. Joseph was lovely. I had time to think.

I fetched a glass of water and ate a banana. I washed the dishes in the sink. Had a quick shower and changed into something that would look good on the webcam. It has become important to dress well for every zoom call. Corners of our living rooms had become our new public spaces. I turned on the lights near my computer.

The call clicked on.

"Hello, how are you? Can you hear me?" I said.

"Hello Greg, how are you?" My therapist said through the computer.

"Good, I just went for a run with Joseph, got in about an hour ago. Feeling good," I replied. "How are you?" I continued.

"Good good, how was the run?" she continued.

"Oh fine, I just stopped at the end at the park bench I used to sit on all the time," I said gingerly. "It was weird, I haven't stopped by it for a long time. It was weird."

"Ok, let's start there then. Why did you think that you stopped there today?" she asked.

"I don't know, I just kinda was going past it on the run, and stopped there. I had no feeling towards it but I sat down and it just kind of twanged me back into all the things that happened. Like the bad stuff that he did." I answered.

I paused for a moment. Was I really about to bring up something that was done with? Why was I thinking about this?

"It is ok to rehash some of the things that happen when you start falling in love with someone new. You want them to know everything about you. Everything you have been through, the good and the bad," She stated.

"What if he sees me as a loser for the things that have happened, I mean I sat at a bench for months crying and wading through the same thoughts like an insane person," I said.

"It wasn't insane, you had to process what happened," she said. "You had to stop and think of things that happened. Remember what he put you through after you moved out? The calls to your friends, trying to get keys to your apartment, contacting Caroline. That was bullying and harassment, Gregory, he bullied you even after he left that note for you. You yourself identified that he was getting satisfaction from seeing you in pain. He even tried to make your work environment uncomfortable for you," she finished.

I was reminded quickly that I still had not told Joseph about the times that Robert showed up to events that I was working in the weeks after the separation. How he had asked me for keys to my new apartment, and how I almost gave him a copy. How he tried to sleep with a handful of my friends. How, although it had been a year and a half, he was still texting me every now and again, sometimes once every two weeks, sometimes once every two months.

We were five minutes into the session and she was dropping the hammer.

"Why don't we do an exercise, let's play out what it would look like if you played into what he wanted. What do you think your life would look like?" she said.

"I guess I would still be unhappy" I mumbled in compliance. "...and in something that made no sense. Staying in a relationship for the appearance and family is the wrong reason, I know that. But, but... What if I could have made it work?" I said, starting to feel emotional.

"What does 'work' look like to you? He was lying to you constantly. How many times did he put your health at risk, he contracted STD after STD. Is that respectful to you or the relationship?" she shifted in her seat and seemed to be stopping herself from speaking. It was hard to read the situation over the computer. "And remember all the things he did to you afterwards. It was truly bad Gregory."

I took a beat.

"I think that I have made the right choices given the circumstances," I replied softly.

It never got easier being reminded of what he had done, and subsequently how I treated myself.

"You sent me an email earlier in the week, why don't we talk about that?" she asked, suddenly relenting.

"Yeah, I have been having more anxiety about the news lately. It has been a year of this pandemic, so I guess that is what the dream I had was about," I started out, grateful for the change in topic.

"You said in this dream that you were rushing to get things done in time, and things were getting in your way?"

"Yes. In the dream all I can really remember is being in a supermarket and trying to get to every aisle, not to buy things but to look at everything that was on the shelves, in case I needed something," I said.

The email I had sent her was rather vague. It was what I could remember of a dream. Nothing more than what I had told her.

"So you are just trying to look at all the options then?" she continued. I nodded. "Right, so given the year we are having, do you think that maybe you have a fear that you have missed out on things that normally would have been happening?" she asked.

"I mean, yeah, but, who doesn't right now? A whole year has been lost to this pandemic, a year of what would have been normal life. But look at this. It's all fucked," I said, exasperated.

"Well, Gregory, it's not all fucked. I think most of the people have done well during this. Remember at the start how scary this was?" she asked.

"Yeah, and it still is. I feel like it is unrelenting. There is nothing to be done, no way of getting this time back. Some people have done the 'get fit' thing. I have gotten in and out of shape like three times during this period. Some people have learnt how to cook, I already know how to cook. Either everyone is lying or I am way the fuck behind," I said, upset that I had just ended a sentence so defeated with my therapist.

We both paused.

"Gregory, you have done something you thought you would never do again. You found love," she said with an airy tone.

It is hard to roll your eyes at someone over Zoom.

"It's not a competition Greg," she said in response to my silence.

"It's not fair. I know I should be grateful that the health of the people I love wasn't too badly affected, but this is just so unfair. A whole year of life, of doing things normally and growing. Using all of the things that I work so hard to get, like a social life, going to the gym, travel, they've all just been taken away. It's just so unfair," I finished.

"I know," she replied in a motherly tone. "I know."

We finished the call as we normally do. I returned to my yoga mat and lay down to stare at the ceiling. These days of boredom, TV, books, Zoom chats, were now becoming insufferable. Nothing in this winter would blunt the feeling of imprisonment. Crimelessly confined to our own homes. Unrelenting from boredom.

GORDON LONG

CHAPTER 14

Joseph and I had been sleeping at each other's apartments shortly after we began dating. Now five months into dating we had a routine, He would stay at mine 2 nights a week, and would stay at his two nights a week. We even had toothbrushes and comfy clothes at each other's homes. We lived on opposite ends of the gay village, only three blocks apart. His style was minimalist, north-facing windows with not a lot of sunlight. My apartment was second-hand furniture and books stacked in piles as 'accent features.' The eleventh month of the lockdowns had us both happy to be in spaces other than our own. I stepped out of his building, closing my coat for the afternoon stroll home.

It was mid-afternoon and Church Street was cold and bustling, the early March air was still cold enough to see your breath in. Despite the cold, there were birds chirping in the afternoon sun. Walking down the street I saw a man huddled on the stoop of a closed bar I frequented before the lockdowns. Seeing homeless people sitting out on the street was a common occurrence now. The pandemic had reduced the capacity of the shelters at the start of the lockdowns, so the homeless population was finding anywhere and any way to stay warm.

This man huddled on the corner was wearing really nice boots.

And a scarf that looked familiar.

I almost walked right past before realizing who it was.

Stuart was sitting with his head in his hands, his face barely visible under his facemask and winter attire.

"Stuart? Babe, what's going on? I almost thought you were... someone else," I said, leaning down, quickly stopping myself from talking more as I realized Stuart was crying. I reached out and put my hand on his shoulder. He tilted his head up, his swollen eyes leading the streaks of tears down his cheeks. He lowered his mask to reveal a split lip. It was still plump and bruised. I knew that type of injury, he had been hit in the face, and recently. I moved my hands towards him, he cowered away. It was strange given the difference in our statures, him large and broadly muscular, me short and lean. The way he moved away from me quickly registered to me like fear.

I sat down next to him.

"Stuart, what happened?" I asked a little more firmly.

He took a breath in.

"I.. We... Ignacio and I, we just... had a fight," he replied.

He was starting to shake, his hands were up under his chin.

"He... got a little carried away and hit me," he continued.

"Where is he?" I asked. I could feel my hands starting to shake. "Did you hit him back?" I quickly finished.

"God no. You know me, I don't do violence or confrontation very well," he replied.

"What happened? Why do you have a cut lip?" I asked

"He just got so upset and he had been drinking. I moved in, towards him. I put my hand on his shoulder because he wouldn't look at me. And then he just swung his elbow into my face," Stuart finished, looking somewhat startled by what he had just said.

"Where is he?" I asked again.

"I think he took off to a friend's house, I just don't want to be at home right now," he replied.

"Ok well, why don't we go to my apartment and get you cleaned up a little bit?" I said.

Silently, we rose from the cold concrete stoop and made our way across the street towards my home. Stuart clung to my arm as we crossed the street, a good level of dramatic effect.

Ignacio had moved into Stuart's apartment after two months of an intense romance. They had been living in Stuart's one-bedroom apartment for three months now. 'Bliss' was the only word Stuart had used to describe his new living arrangements.

Opening my front door, we took off all our winter clothes. The ritual of undressing at a door in the Canadian winter is always rather comforting. Stuart gave a small shudder as he made his way in his jogging pants and what looked like a thin pyjama top to my radiator. I moved to the kitchen to turn on the kettle.

In the bathroom, I wet a cloth in warm water and retrieved antiseptic ointment for his face. I purposefully sanitized my hands in front of Stuart.

"Let's get a quick look at that lip," I said.

I moved towards Stuart and he obliged, grateful to be taken care of. I put the wet cloth up against his injury to wipe away the dried blood.

"He really clocked you, huh?" I said.

A thought crossed my mind and I paused. "Should we take photos of this?" I asked.

"Does this look like something I want to remember?" Stuart said.

I started shaking my head, "No, like if you need photo evidence for the police. This is assault," I finished, looking into Stuart's eyes, trying to gauge a response.

The colour in Stuart's face changed, he blushed, then a look of steeliness came over his eyes. He lowered his head and looked down into his hands, he let out a small groan…

"Oh, I hadn't thought of that, no I couldn't, he would get deported back to Brazil. It's all a mess, no Greg, I just couldn't," he finished.

"I am not saying that you have to report him, I am just saying that maybe we should take some photos, just in case. There is always the option to do nothing about this, but the reality might be different for you in a few days." I concluded.

Wordlessly I reached for my phone, and saw a text from Anthony that read 'we need to talk, ASAP.' I dismissed the notification and opened the camera app.

Focusing in on something grotesque, like a friend's face, damaged like this was a little much to bear. Normally I was taking pictures of food, books and plants. Dried blood, on a lip that normally spoke sweet and friendly words to me, stirred up despair. I stopped myself from crying as I gently wiped the blood off his face and neck, watching as the swelling started to grow.

"What were you doing out on the street like that? So far down the road from your house?" I asked.

"After he left the apartment, I left too. I didn't want to stay there, I just wanted to get out for a bit," Stuart replied.

"And you just sat in the cold, on the stoop of a closed nightclub in the afternoon? On the cold side of the street?" I asked.

"Yeah, I just didn't want to be around anything nice, I didn't want to associate what had just happened with anything good that was around me. I needed this to be ugly. I needed to separate this from the rest of my life," Stuart finished.

I took a beat. It was very typical of Stuart to overthink the moment. To think about how to make sure his positivity, normally infectious, would not be damaged.

The stovetop kettle started whistling as I finished applying ointment to Stuart's lip. He was starting to look less like someone having a bad day. Moving into the kitchen I made a pot of tea, adding milk and sugar. After people have been a little rustled, they tend to need a little sugar in their tea. A trick I had learnt from my mother.

I sat back down on the couch next to Stuart. His head leaning against the wall, a small tear rolling down his face.

"I am just so sick of all this, I date someone and they seem so great, and then I just end up heartbroken," he said defeatedly.

"Stuart, you have so much to offer the world, you are worthy of finding love, this is just the process sometimes," I said quickly, cringing at my choice in words. My friend was having a bad day, and all I could offer was fortune cookie comfort. I repositioned myself on the couch.

"Look Stu, what happened today is not normal, and it fucking sucks. You deserve better than that. There is a lot to be said for how hard this is. You are gay, that leaves you with ten percent of the population. Half of that, aren't even the same gender. So then you have five percent. Then there is location. Age is a factor too..." I trailed off.

"Is this supposed to make me feel better?" Stuart meekly said.

"No, no, it's just that, well... I think that limiting yourself to a certain demographic of men is going to set you up for failure. You have exclusively dated a certain type of guy, always Latino, always younger than you by a year or two. If that is all you are interested in, and you have exhausted that population in this city, then maybe it's time to broaden the group," I said gingerly. The words falling out of me with an even pace. "If you think that what you are doing is working then there wouldn't be a problem, right?" I finished.

My phone clicked again. It was a text from Anthony, 'dude, you need to call me.' I turned my phone down on the coffee table.

"Stuart, you are an amazingly dynamic man, you are one of the most positive and creative people I have ever met. You are worthy of love. I am just saying that relationships and love are not always a straight line." I concluded.

My phone started ringing. It was Anthony, I placed the phone down on the table ignoring the call.

"Who is trying to call you?" Stuart asked.

"Anthony, he has been trying to get a hold of me for the last hour," I replied, looking at my vibrating phone on the coffee table.

"You should answer, it might be important," Stuart said. As the phone stopped vibrating.

"I'll call him back later. I think we should spend some time discussing what to do next. Does Ignacio have a key to your place? Could you ask for it back or should we call a locksmith?" I asked.

The phone started ringing, it was Anthony again.

"I think you should answer that," Stuart said.

I got up and walked to the hallway to answer the call.

"Anthony, this just isn't a good time bud, what's up?" I said into the phone.

"Mate, are you alone right now, where are you?" Anthony asked. His voice had an urgency I had only heard a couple of times.

"I am at home, Stuart is here, he has had a terrible day, can I give you a call in a-" Anthony cut me off.

"Look I need you to know that this is going to be ok, I am heading towards you right now, but please sit down," Anthony said, I could tell that he was driving and had me on Bluetooth.

I silently walked down the hallway into the bedroom and sat on the end of my bed.

"Ant, what's going on?" I asked, I could feel my throat getting dry and my heart flutter.

"Are you sitting down?" Anthony asked. "Yes," I replied.

"Mate, this isn't easy to tell you," Anthony continued.

"Just spit it out Anthony, what happened, what did you do?" I said, annoyed.

Anthony took a breath in. "Robert is dead," he said over the phone.

I felt my stomach turn the same way it does when I am anxious. I felt a light constant thud on the side of my temple. My ears felt hot.

"Nah. What?" I said, hoping I had misheard him.

"I am so sorry that I am telling you this like this, but I am on my way and wanted to make sure you are ok and heard it from me," he said.

"Wait, what, how, how do you know this?" I asked.

"His sister called me, they didn't have your number after you changed it last year," he replied.

"What the fuck Ant, what the fuck, what do I do? What should I do?" I said breathlessly.

Stuart was standing at the door. "Greg what's happening?" he asked.

I stared at Stuart. He looked back at me, bewildered. I passed him the phone. He raised it to his ear, "hello, Anthony?" he said.

I watched Stuart's face as he turned from the wall to look at me. He suddenly looked scared. "How far away are you?" he said into the phone. Not long after he hung up the phone and sat down on the bed next to me.

"Darling, I have no words, I... I don't know what to say," Stuart said blankly.

I looked at myself in the reflection of the mirror near my door. I didn't recognize myself.

"What do I do?" I asked Stuart in a pleading tone.

He looked at me and shook his head.

My mind raced. Why was Robert dead? What happened? When did this happen? What does this mean for his family, do his parents in Quebec know? Does his aunt and uncle in Ontario know? Do some of his friends know? What did he die of, did he kill himself? Was this real? Was Anthony playing a joke? Would Anthony arrive at my door with Robert in tow, and they were trying to pull off some bad joke? Why was he dead? Should I be crying right now? When was the last time I had spoken to him? When was the last time I cried over him?

Stuart put his arm around my shoulder. I got up and moved toward the hallway. I had made tea and suddenly, I was thirsty. I felt a sense of calm hollowness. Stuart followed as I sat down on my couch.

I picked up a cup of tea, it burnt my tongue as I sipped it. My face scrunched up. My tongue hurt. My eyes squinted.

"Are you ok Greg?" Stuart said softly to me.

I let out a whimper. "I hurt my tongue," I said meekly as my breathing changed. I was fighting back a sob. It came out on its own. It was louder than I thought. My whole body started shuddering as Stuart leaned in and put his arms around me. His long arms wrapped around my whole body, pulling me from the comfort of my seat. He held me so tightly it felt like he was trying to squeeze the sob out.

I began to cry loudly.

Stuart began to cry too. He finally let go of the embrace and we both reclined into the couch, I was staring blankly at the ceiling.

Some time passed. I was non-verbal. Stuart asked me some questions, each time he did it sounded shallower and shallower in my ears.

Anthony walked into my apartment, went straight to the fridge then joined Stuart and I in the living room. He pulled up a chair and sat facing us, his elbows resting on his knees, slouched forward as if he was a coach about to give the game-saving speech.

"Ok, here is what I know. He went into the hospital three days ago, he was trying to treat his Covid symptoms at home, and because he still lives alone, in that huge house, no one had checked up on him in a week or so. He just kept ordering food to the house or I guess he just wasn't eating, I don't know," Anthony said.

"He had Covid? Fuck. What the fuck?" I muttered.

"He was admitted three days ago to the Covid ward after he called himself an ambulance... he was put on a ventilator shortly after that. Then he died early the next morning. He was just too far gone," Anthony said, very matter of factly. "His family in Quebec were notified the following day, which was yesterday, and they called me about an hour ago because they couldn't get through to you," he concluded.

There was silence in the room.

"What hospital was he in?" I asked.

"Toronto General, I believe," Anthony said. Clearly, he was fighting back tears too. "I am so sorry mate, I just... I am so sorry," he sputtered out, putting his hands up over his eyes. His shoulders arching over him as he started to cry.

I looked at Anthony, I still hadn't moved. Stuart rose from the couch and moved towards Anthony and put his hands on his shoulders. Leaning down, he pulled Anthony into a tight hug. I could see the discomfort in Anthony's eyes as he stared at me, signalling that he wanted out of this very tight hug. I pointed to my lip, staring at Anthony then pointed to Stuart. Anthony had a look of question before realizing what I was gesturing.

"What happened to your lip?" Anthony said.

The hug was disengaged.

"Oh, I just... it has been a bit of a morning," Stuart replied.

"How does the other guy look?" Anthony said with a chuckle, clearing the tears away from the corners of his eyes.

Stuart gave a slight chuckle. "It was a bad morning." They looked at one another sweetly.

They both turned and looked at me. Anthony stood up from his chair and headed into the kitchen. I heard the fridge open. I heard the unmistakable clinking of beer bottles and caps being removed. Anthony returned to the living room as Stuart sat down.

Anthony handed us each a bottle of beer and returned to his chair while he took a swig.

"I need to make some calls to his family, especially his mom, Martha," I said, finishing my sip.

"No, you don't have to, unless you want to," Stuart said.

"Last time I spoke to his mom was in January, she sent me a card for my birthday and I called her to thank her. She is a lovely woman and was always great to me. I should call her," I concluded.

"Are you sure?" Stuart asked again.

"Look, this situation is brutal, there is no right or wrong in this, Greg, if you want to do something, do it. If you want to do nothing then that's fine too." Anthony said.

"I will call them in a bit. I was in their family for seven years, I just don't know what to say right now. I need to think about this. Oh man, this is fucked..." I slowly started to cry again. I placed my beer on the table. Stuart leaned into me. I put a hand on his shoulder, trying subversively to stop another hug. The action of which was not lost on Anthony. He looked at me and smiled, almost laughing as the corners of his mouth turned upwards.

"Nope," I said loudly, without thinking. Stuart retracted a little and looked at me. I leaned into him, putting my shoulder inside his. Realizing that comfort needs comfort, he returned the gesture and pulled me into a soft embrace. Anthony seemed to not know where to look.

"How do I talk to Joseph about this?" I asked the room.

No answer was given. We sat in silence.

Finishing our beers, Anthony fetched more. As he returned, Stuart stood up.
"Sorry, but I have to go. I have so many things to get done today," Stuart said, starting towards the door. I followed him into the foyer. He started dressing for the outside, it was starting to get dark now.

"Ok love, call me if you need anything," Stuart said.

"Are you going to call a locksmith?" I asked.

"There is a chain lock on the inside of the door, I doubt he will have been back there in the last few hours," Stuart said as he opened the door, putting on his mask. "Bye Anthony!" he called out.

I walked back into the living room, Anthony was sitting on the couch. The three fresh beers sat on the coffee table.

"I really don't have any advice. How do you feel?" He said, taking a swig of the new bottle.

"I feel numb. I just don't know how to quantify it. What do you do when someone that you used to love, who treated you terribly for a few years, dies of the fucking current plague?" I said. Another tear welling in the corner of my eye.

Anthony drew his breath between his teeth loudly and sighed. "I don't know," he whispered while taking a sip of beer.

The sun fell behind the horizon, sunlight was now absent. The blue wall in my apartment cast a sombre tone in the twilight. I lit two lamps in the living room and sat back down on the couch.

"I should call them," I said. Anthony locked eyes with me and he didn't answer.

I picked up my phone and dialled the number I had committed to memory.

Three rings. Maybe I should just hang up.

"Hello?" It was Alfred. Robert's father.

"Hi, Al, it's Greg, I just got the call," I said, suddenly choking up.

"Ah yes, terrible business. We are not well over it, very not well. I'll put Martha on..." I listened to him put the phone to his chest. "Martha, it's Gregory, he has called to talk to you I am guessing."

There was rustling on the line.

I heard Martha clear her throat. "Hello, Greg darling?"

"Hi Martha. I... I am so sorry" I said, losing my emotion during the sentence. I held the receiver of my cell phone away from my head.

"It all 'appened so quickly Greg, my baby, my baby boy," she said in her light French Canadian twang.

I did not know what to say. "How are you?" I asked, instantly regretting the question.

I heard her take a shallow breath in.

"It was just so sudden, one minute he was telling us he had a cold, he didn't think it was the corona because he could still smell 'is supper. Then I got a call from the hospital a few days later. It is almost not even a real thing," she concluded.

I heard another rustling on the receiver.

"Greg? We have to do some things here, we might need your help, we don't know. We are all the way down here in Montreal you see," Alfred said.

"Of course, whatever you need. Al, what do you need?" I asked.

"Well, we are not sure yet, but we will need someone like you down there to help out getting him home, and getting all his things back to us so we can figure out what to do with it all," Al said.

Again, I had to hold the receiver away from my face as I wept. Anthony was looking at me with a puzzled look.

"Yep, I can help." I said into the receiver, trying to hold back my tears.

"Thank you, Greg, God bless," Alfred finished.

THE DETERMINIST

"Please tell Martha she can call me whenever she needs, and do not hesitate to do so yourself," I finished.

"Ok, God bless" Alfred finished.

The phone clicked off.

I turned to Anthony. "That was the hardest phone call I think I have ever had to make. I hated that," I started sobbing as I finished the sentence.

Anthony nodded at me. He took a sip of his beer. Draining it. "Cannot imagine, mate," he said.

We sat in silence for a few moments. "Are you ok?" Anthony asked.

"No," I replied.

CHAPTER 15

Winding up through the annals of the parking garage was like second nature at this point. Over the years I had rented so many cars from this specific car agency, in the third sub-basement in an office tower downtown, that their garage was now easy to navigate. Given that it was a Saturday morning during the pandemic, the lot was deserted. The car lurched up the series of left turns.

As I broached out onto Front street, the sky was grey. I looked to the right, Joseph and Anthony were waiting on the corner. They had our bags, the box of Robert's things that didn't make it into the initial truck his sister drove down, our suit bags and coffee. They made their way towards the car, I popped the trunk and got out to help them load everything in. Anthony climbed into the back seat as Joseph sat in the front passenger seat.

"Alright?" I said as I adjusted the mirrors on the side panel.

Anthony leaned forward and put a hand on my shoulder, and locked eyes with me in the rear vision mirror. "You still have the parking brake on…" he said in a low voice.

THE DETERMINIST

I pressed the parking brake lever with my left foot. Feeling like a fool, of course the car was lurching, and of course when there were bell tones ringing, I still felt so numb that they had not registered.

We passed a few intersections, turning the car onto the highway.

"It's always amazed me that within twenty minutes you can be outside Toronto," I said, absentmindedly.

Neither Joseph nor Anthony replied.

The 400 highway between Toronto and Montreal was quiet. I looked over to Joseph, whose head was starting to sleepily bob as the car moved. Anthony was laying down on the backseat, using bags as a pillow, reading a book.

As I drove, flashbacks from times I had driven this highway with Robert, to his parents' home in Brossard and to Montreal, started to play in my mind.

That time we stopped in Gananoque on a whim and took a ferry boat through the Thousand Islands. The time we rolled down the windows and threw the inedible cookies his mother had made at snowbanks, making a game of who could throw the farthest. The times we had stopped on the highway rest stops to fool around on the way home from family visits, where we had been in separate rooms the whole time.

It had been six days since Anthony told me that Robert was dead. The day I found out, it was difficult telling Joseph. What had been harder was the influx of good memories from my relationship with Robert. Yes, we had existed once, happily together. But that was not what the last few years had been. It was like my brain was playing a strange and stupid trick on me. I was in a relationship and in love with Joseph, but now that Robert had died, and so suddenly, I could only think of the times we were happy. I hated this. These thoughts felt intrusive. They made me squirm.

Joseph roused as we neared the Quebec border.

"What time is it? Where are we?" he asked, wiping away the drool from the side of his mouth.

"We are about two hours from Montreal, we should take a break soon, I need to pee," I said, putting my hand on his knee.

He turned to me and smiled.

"Thank you for coming," I said to him, softly, not wanting Anthony to hear me.

He reached over and put his hand behind my neck, rubbing the lower part of my head.

"Of course, this is a rough time," he said. "And yeah, I need to stop too, how long until we reach the rest stop?" he finished.

"Five minutes-ish…" I said vaguely.

After a few moments, I saw the turnoff to the rest stop. 'Last OnRoute stop' the sign read.

I veered off the highway. Anthony sat up in the back seat. "Thank fuck, I am starving," he proclaimed.

After parking the car the three of us made our way into the rest stop. There was no lineup for the washroom, and all the seating areas had been taped off, you weren't allowed to sit down, as per the provincial lockdowns. After using the washrooms and stocking up on Tim's doughnuts and coffee we started back to the car.

"How much longer until we are in Montreal?" Joseph asked again.

"Around two hours, but we have to stop at the parents' place first, in Broussard. It's just twenty minutes south of Montreal," I replied. Hoping that Joseph would not catch onto the fact that I just referred to Robert's parents' home as 'the parents'.'

Leading our way back to the car, I felt myself starting to cry. I had stopped in this very rest stop so many times over the years with Robert. I didn't want to let on to the other two that I was feeling like this. I put my sunglasses on, hoping to cover the tears in my eyes. As we reached the car, there was no stopping what was about to happen. I unlocked the car and put my coffee in the cupholder.

"I'll be right back," I said. Turning quickly as Joseph looked at me. Hoping he wouldn't notice me crying. Walking past the other cars I made it back to the rest stop, and into a bathroom stall.

I leant against the stall and wiped the tears from my eyes. I took a moment to gather myself. Took a few deep breaths. I walked out of the stall and towards the washbasins. Joseph entered the washrooms.

"Babe, are you ok?" Joseph asked.

"Yeah, I just... I just got a little overwhelmed just then." I replied, hoping he would not see the fact that I had been crying.

"It's going to be a tough few days," Joseph said.

I felt like he had said that to me a thousand times in the last week. He had started coming over to my home every morning before he started work to check on me. He would listen to me at night when I would express how I felt. After the initial therapy session I had, he was waiting for me with takeout and a bottle of wine.

He had been truly supportive and lovely over the last week, but I wish he would stop telling me that 'it was going to be rough' and looking at me like he did some days, like I might start a fire in my apartment or something.

Joseph put his hand on my shoulder. "Why don't you ask Anthony to drive the rest of the way?" he proposed.

"Yeah, maybe I should," I concluded.

Joseph and I made our way back to the car to ask Anthony to drive, he obliged and moved into the driver's seat. I went into the backseat and nestled into the groove that Anthony had made in the luggage.

As we moved forward, I checked my phone every so often. Kelsey, Robert's sister, had been messaging me. 'How far away are you guys?'

THE DETERMINIST

'Not too far, about another hour from Brossard, can you let Al and Martha know?' I replied.

The next hour of driving passed without any concern. A few absent-minded conversations between Joseph and Anthony that I didn't listen to.

As we wound off the highway and into the suburb near Robert's parents' home, I felt a jab of anxiety. It was strange to have these moments, they had been fluttering through me over the last week. The reality of what was happening had started to filter into me at strange moments.

Suddenly the seatbelt across my chest felt constricting. My breathing changed.

"It's just up here on the left... right?" Anthony asked. The feelings of anxiety twisted in me as I realized I had to answer.

"Yeah, it's the next left then at the end of the street," I replied. Trying not to let on that my throat was dry and my voice felt tight.

The car slowed as we approached the home. Anthony had been here once years ago when we were all in Montreal for a weekend. He pulled the car up on the sidewalk. I opened the car door and walked around to the trunk. Anthony had not even turned the car off yet. I opened the trunk and retrieved the box of things that Martha had requested I set aside.

Walking up to the front door I felt a small flutter in my chest again. I saw flowers, Tupperware dishes and cake tins, along with cards of condolence on the front step. I added the box to the area, on top of a bench. I saw the drapes move out of the corner of my eye, I looked up to see Martha, teary-eyed looking at me. My eyes started to flood with tears. I backed away from the door as she unlatched the lock from the inside. She opened the door while putting on a facemask.

"Hi Greg, I am so glad you came," Martha said, muffled through her facemask. "Al is still in bed, he hasn't been getting up too quickly over the last week, I'd invite you in, but given the quarantine, lockdowns, whatever they are calling it now..." she trailed off.

"How are you?" I asked. Moving myself a small step closer to her.

I could tell that behind her eyes, Martha was waging something with herself. In one fast and deliberate motion, she stepped forward and pulled me into an embrace.

I felt her whole body sigh and then start to shake. Her frail frame felt weak in my arms. She began to cry. Sobbing onto my shoulder.

"My boy..." she wept in a pleading tone.

I looked inside the house, I felt my body tense up and then a moment of relief to see Robert walking towards me. But it wasn't Robert. His father and he shared the same face, the same stature. Alfred had risen from bed and was coming to console his wife.

"Oh 'ello Greg" Alfred said as he put his hands on Martha's shoulders. "C'mon dear, c'mon," he said, pulling her away from me.

I stood and watched as the elderly couple formed their stance together.

"How was the drive?" Alfred asked.

"Easy, Anthony drove the last of it," I said.

"Good of Anthony to come too, that is good, and I guess that fellow in the front seat is your friend too?" Alfred asked.

"Yeah, Joseph. He came," I started to speak, stopping myself as I realized I hadn't told them that I had met someone new... "He came too," I said to Alfred.

Martha continued to sob into Alfred's shoulder. Collecting herself, she turned to me.

"I think I will see you tomorrow, yes, at the church, then to the interment?" Martha asked.

"Yes, I will be there, I am staying at an apartment I rented near Kelsey's house," I replied.

"Well we better get back to it, we need to rest up for tomorrow. See you then Greg," Alfred said with a strained voice, his face sombre and sallow.

They turned into the foyer of their home and Alfred reached back to close the door behind him. "Bye Greg," he said once more, and the door began to close.

I walked back to the car, Anthony was standing out by the driver's seat.

"So?" he asked.

"Let's go, I want to leave," I replied, opening the car door and sitting back in the groove created by the previous few hours of resting.

"Are you ok babe?" Joseph asked, turning his body from the front passenger seat.

"I want to leave, I want to go. Anthony.... Ant, can you just drive. I need to get out of here," I said, hoping I wasn't sounding too dramatic.

Anthony started the car and eased us up the residential street.

"How far away is this apartment?" Anthony asked. Opening a map app on my phone I directed him to the place we would be sleeping.

As there was a lockdown in Montreal as well, there weren't too many cars out on the roads. We snaked our way through the downtown and made it to the apartment with ease.

It was a two-bedroom apartment, Anthony taking the smaller room and Joseph and I taking the larger bed. I lay down on top of the comforter.

"I knew that was going to be hard, but oh my fucking god, that was brutal," I said to Joseph "I never imagined I would see them like that. I feel so useless," I finished.

"You're not useless. This is shit. This is going to be shit," Joseph replied.

"I couldn't imagine what they are thinking right now. Burying your son, and the only people you are allowed to have in the room are the people on a pre-approved list because the virus that killed your son could kill all of the people attending," I said.

Joseph lay down next to me.

"What did you say to them?" Joseph asked.

"I... I don't remember... Well, like, when I spoke to them last week it was all logistics about how to organize the body and his stuff. Then Kelsey came to Toronto, so I didn't need to talk to them anymore. Today I just kinda asked them how they were," I said.

"And, how were they?" Joseph asked. "Not good," I quickly replied.

"I am starving, and nothing is really open here because of the lockdowns, we have to go to a supermarket or get take-out," I said.

Joseph stayed at the apartment to shower while Anthony and I meandered up the street. The apartment I had booked was close to the intersection of St Urbain and St Catherines, normally a bustling pocket of downtown Montreal. Now the streets were quieter. We made our way into a dépanneur. We split up and picked a few things off the shelves and met again at the cash register.

"What time are we meeting with Kelsey tonight?" Anthony asked.

"I don't know. I have to call her. I'll do it when we get back to the apartment," I said.

Leaving the store, I looked at what we had bought. Sandwiches, beef jerky, apples, energy bars and a large bottle of wine. Anthony reached into the bag, pulled out a sandwich, lowered his face mask and started to eat it as we were walking down the street.

It was now 3 pm. I was feeling tired. I hadn't been sleeping well over the last few nights.

We walked in to see Joseph was watching the news on his iPad, adhering to the daily ritual of tuning in to find out how many positive cases had been reported in the country. How many cases per province. How many deaths today. I had not looked at all over the last week, but Joseph had told me about the recent outbreaks.

"Hungry, babe?" I asked Joseph.

Anthony uncorked the bottle of wine and poured three glasses while I lay out the food on the small table in the kitchen.

The three of us sat. Eating in silence, Anthony filled my wine glass when I finished it.

"Ok so, tonight we should meet up with Kelsey, I know she will be wanting to see you, Anthony," I started "And she is going to love you babe," I turned to Joseph. "Then tomorrow, I need to be at the church at 11 am. Then we drive to the cemetery, then

THE DETERMINIST

Kelsey wants to have some people over to meet-up in her garden. Does that sound good to you guys?" I finished. They both nodded, chewing through their sandwiches.

I had gone over this plan with Joseph and Anthony individually, but saying it out loud again made it feel more normal. Like I was in control of at least this one run of events.

I felt badly that the whole trip was going to be centred around the funeral for my ex. My new boyfriend, sitting listening to the plans that had been made.

My phone started ringing. It was Kelsey. I answered and got up from the table.

"Hi Kels, how are you?" I said into the receiver. Kelsey and I had always got along very well, for years my trips to Montreal were punctuated with her and I escaping from the family to go to a bar, or to a cabaret show.

"Hi Greg, how was the drive? Mum told me she saw you," she said.
"Drive was fine, we are all here in one piece. What time should we meet up?" I asked.

"Oh come over any time. I am fine to have you guys in the house, I don't think there is much of a risk there, or we can sit out in the backyard if you prefer," she said to me.

"Yeah, I think the backyard would be smarter, we have been travelling all day, and, I mean it's not like if any of us caught it, it would be too bad..." I stopped myself from completing the sentence. I had stopped saying that I wasn't scared of catching the virus, just scared of passing it on. Robert was a strong man, and it took him down quickly.

"Well, yeah, maybe we should just stick to the back garden then," she said. "I'll open some wine when you guys get here," she finished.

"Can I bring anything?" I asked.

"No, no. Just come when you are ready," she said flatly.

"Ok we will be there in about an hour," I said finishing the call.

After about half an hour, the three of us left the apartment, dressed in our warmest clothes to walk the frosty ten minutes to Kelsey's house.

We reached Kelsey's home, a classic Montreal terrace house, thin and long, with a back entrance and a street-front entrance. Very chic and cool.

We walked around the laneway and up to her back garden. Kelsey was sitting on the small wooden deck at her back door. She descended the stairs to come and sit with us. I could see from the red wine stains around her mouth she had been drinking. She looked understandably terrible.

"Hi Kels, this is Joseph," I said, gesturing towards him.

"Ah yes, Greg has told me about you, good to meet you," she said, feigning a smile.

Anthony looked as if he was about to defuse a bomb. The three of us advanced towards the chairs Kelsey had put out in the back garden.

She went back inside and came out with 3 more glasses and a fresh bottle of wine. Joseph, who was from a family of people who didn't drink, looked at me with worried eyes.

"Just hold on to it, she won't notice," I whispered to Joseph.

The four of us sat and chatted, Anthony took the lead by telling Kelsey everything he had been doing since they last saw each other a few years before.

Joseph started sipping from his wine glass and I watched as he started to get a little wobbly in his seat. The four of us were starting to sound a little drunk.

After about 90 minutes and another bottle of wine, I turned to Kelsey. "Ok, so tomorrow morning we meet at 11 am at the church near your parents' house for the service, then we all go over to the cemetery, then meet back here right?"

Kelsey gave me a sordid look. "Still always planning huh. Yes, that is the plan Greg," she muttered out the last few words of the sentence.

After a few moments of saying our goodbyes, we made our way across the back garden out onto the street. It was cold and damp and the three of us started walking, drunkenly, back to the apartment.

***

The three of us sat in the car, dressed in suits and drinking Mcdonald's coffee. The sky was a brilliant blue. I could hear the words of my mother, repeating in my mind. 'One foot in front of the other, chin up.'

The car park started to fill, I saw some vehicles that I recognized, Robert's aunt from Cornwall, who must have driven in, his cousin Micheal who was identical to Robert, except for the mop of curly hair. His cousin Kate, a silly blonde woman who always said the wrong thing. And finally, the grey Jetta brought Martha and Albert.

They all filtered in by the time we had finished our coffee.

I looked at my watch. It was time to put on our masks and approach the church. Anthony opened his door and stepped out. I turned to Joseph. He already had his mask on, fogging up his glasses.

"I love you, and I don't know what I did to deserve you, but I am so grateful for you," I said as I pulled down his mask and kissed him.

"I got you," he said. Then turned. "Remember today will happen with or without you. Be as involved as you want," he said.

I sat for another moment in the car, Joseph's words thudding in my ears like a bomb blast. As involved as I want?

I stepped out of the car, took a deep breath and put my mask on.

THE DETERMINIST

Walking up to the group that had now formed in front of the church, I approached Alfred. He was holding himself up strongly.

"Ah, Greg, you look good in your suit," he said awkwardly.

Not knowing what to say, I nodded at him and proceeded into the church.

Past the foyer of the old church were two large doors. Decades of paint and lacquer fortified these doors, even the bolts had a consistent sheen with the wood.

I pulled open the left handle of the door, and stepped into the grandeur of the church. It was an old bluestone, with green carpets and maple pews. I was never religious, but there was a charm to churches that made you feel small in a way even a mountain couldn't match. My eyes followed down the center of the division in pews, to the rectory. On the chancel was a metal scissor frame holding up the long coffin. To the right of it was a wreath, to the left was a large picture of Robert.

I had prepared myself for this. I had prepared myself for the moment of being in the same building as his dead body. None of that was useful at this moment.

Behind me, the large door creaked open again. It was Anthony.

"They are telling us we can't come in, the church can only have 25 people in it because of the lockdown," Anthony said with a panicked look in his eyes.

I felt exhausted by the comment. I didn't want to be dealing with this. I wanted to be sitting in the front row of the church with the other mourners, my previous in-laws, my past family. I wanted to cry, and then leave and cry some more. I just wanted all of this to be over.

"What?" I asked. Trying my best to have a lousy, queried look.

Anthony looked at me and gestured. "I think you need to come out here, Joseph is out there by himself mate," he concluded.

The issue was not lost on me. I looked back towards the back of the church, to where he lay, in his closed coffin, next to a picture of him smiling, and some flowers he would have hated.

I made an audible breath out. "Ok, yeah, ok. How bad is it?" I asked.

"You just need to show up out there, mate," Anthony said back to me.

I walked out into the parking lot. Kelsey was standing to the side, in a chic black gown. I moved towards her. As I approached, I saw Joseph lingering behind her.

"Thought this one looked lost," Kelsey said, as she pulled Joseph close to her.

I didn't know how to respond. I remained silent.

There was a hubbub to my right.

"Yes, So, we can only admit those invited by the family. I know this is a difficult day but we need to remain compliant with the current restrictions," a tall man in a suit recited, while standing close to Martha and Albert.

Kelsey grabbed Joseph, Anthony and I by the hands and led us to the front steps of the church. Placing us at the side of the front doors, she stepped back out towards her parents, and like a sheep herder gestured them towards the doors, she then made her way into the crowd and came back with an older lady, who I recognized as Susan, Robert's aunt. Kelsey was the proactive force required when everybody else was immobilized by grief.

Susan was looking down, then looked up and saw me. She locked eyes. I could feel the heat coming out of her stare.

Joseph's hand reached around the back of my suit jacket, resting his hand on my lower back. His hand then wrapped around my fingers tightly. I looked at him and he motioned with his head towards the door, as Martha and Alfred were starting into the foyer. We followed.

Behind the large lacquered doors that I had just been behind, I watched as Martha was being held up by Albert, they slowly staggered down the aisle, towards the front pew. I could inaudibly sense the voice of Martha. Her worst fears as a mother recognized, not even her husband of fifty years could console her.

Behind Joseph and I was Kelsey, followed by Anthony and Susan. A small sniffle of defeat came out of Kelsey. I broke from Joseph's clutches, to put my arm under her shoulder and catch her just as she started to cry.

Kelsey and I both straightened up. We continued forward. I saw Joseph sit down in a pew behind the front. I walked with Kelsey up to the front pew to meet her parents. She sat down. I lent in to hug her. As I went to move away, back to Joseph, Kelsey pulled on my arm. She pulled me down into the seat next to her. Sitting fourth in mourning, with the family.

I looked around to see Joseph and Anthony sitting together in the pew behind me. Neither of them was looking in my direction. I looked forward. I could hear people being ushered in.
I looked at the flowers on the easel.
"Who decided on pink and white?" I asked Kelsey.

Kelsey turned to me with a smile.

"When Rob was little, he used to get bullied for picking flowers, but he would come home, with all these lovely bunches of wildflowers. God knows where he got them from. He pressed them for a few years. He just loved pink and white flowers," she tearfully revealed.

I stared at her.

How had I been in such an intimate relationship with someone for so many years, and never known this? Robert had told me he hated flowers. The decor theme of most of our apartments was hockey colours and the occasional picture from an adventure. I had never seen Robert, the amateur florist.

I sunk back into the pew. New, hotter tears were forming in my eyes. New ones that hadn't arrived before. How was there more to him that I didn't know? Why was I only learning about it now?

"Good morning everyone, and thank you for making the time to be here today," the priest started, lowering his face mask.

THE DETERMINIST

I sat listening to the ceremony, it was different than in the movies. There was no grand eulogy. The priest read out a statement from Martha and Alfred.

During the final remarks, we were discouraged from embracing. And then the time came at the end of the priest's sermon. The moment I'd been dreading, but also dutifully anticipating. Kelsey grabbed my hand and stood up. I followed her stance, running my hands down my suit to flatten it out. As Kelsey and I walked toward the chancel, Micheal and another two of Robert's cousins stood in their pews, following.

As we all assembled around the front of the casket, Albert stood. A stoic look in his eyes as he lumbered up to join us.

We all lined up and looked at the funeral director. I had been asked about my height in an email before the service. I knew that I was to stand at the foot end, as a smaller person. Kelsey stood on the other side of the coffin from me.

"Ok, so everyone down, and bend your shoulder under the frame" the funeral director quietly instructed us.

I couldn't see behind me, but I assumed that we were all moving at the same time.

I heard a slight groan from behind me, as the coffin edged its way up onto our shoulders, lopsided by our difference in heights.

The metal frame was removed from under us behind the coffin. In front of me, the assistant to the funeral director appeared. She locked eyes with me, then locked eyes with Kelsey. Her hands were held up around her face like she was performing a spell. Twisting her fingers in a 'come hither' motion.

We, as a unit, started to move forward. I felt Kelsey's hand touching my upper arm, I couldn't look at her, but I felt her arm. I felt her emotion and struggle. My shoulder hurt under the weight of the coffin. The edge was digging into my neck.

'Don't fail this' kept going through my head. Tears welled in my eyes as we made our way down the church, to the now opened doors.

I was walking down the aisle on the opposite side from Joseph and Anthony. A quick panic went through my head as I realized they wanted us to carry this coffin down the steep front steps. What if we stumbled?

As we passed the lacquered doors the metal frame reappeared. The assistant directed us to put the coffin down on it. Kelsey and I first, followed by the larger men at the back.

Kelsey stood fast next to the coffin. I remained in my place too. The assistant then directed us to walk the coffin on its metal frame and wheels to the side ramp, where the coffin was maneuvered, with each of the pallbearers down the slightly curved ramp.

A black Cadillac hearse was waiting with its back door wide open, lined with more flowers.
As we approached it. Kelsey gave out a whimper. She and I peeled away from the coffin.

THE DETERMINIST

I watched Alfred put his hands on the coffin, as the assistant and the hearse driver aligned it with the back scaffolding, jolting it into place. A sudden movement that was jarring.

"No, not like that, there... No, have some dignity with it. That's my boy," Alfred said, with a weakness in the last word of his sentence. A pain I had never heard before.

Micheal, Robert's cousin, put his large arms around Alfred.

"It's just that... that they don't even do it right sometimes, no respect...NO RESPECT!" Alfred continued.

Kelsey moved toward her father. He collapsed into her and started crying. I had never seen Alfred lose his cool.

As the assistant and the hearse driver were wordlessly closing up the vehicle, the crowd started to pour out of the church.

Shortly after the bulk of Robert's family had filtered out into the parking lot, I saw Joseph. He was clutching a copy of the order of service and looking self-conscious. Anthony appeared behind him helping Martha down the steps.

As most of the family made their way to their cars, Joseph, Anthony and I surrounded our rental car. Anthony in the driver's seat. Joseph in the front passenger. Me in the back. Anthony turned on the engine.

"What do we do now?" Anthony asked.

"We wait for the hearse to go, then we follow it with our hazard lights on," said Joseph.

I was surprised by how clear and correct he was. From the look Anthony gave, so was he.

We sat for a few moments. Then, slowly the stream of cars started to follow the hearse.

We drove in silence behind someone who we didn't know, six cars behind the hearse.

We arrived at the cemetery.

After parking, I looked forward to see that the back of the hearse had been opened. I felt a pang of panic, they wouldn't move him to the ground without me? Maybe during the drive, Alfred decided that I, the ex, was not the right person to be moving his son. Maybe during the drive, Alfred and Martha decided that their son deserved better than to have me as his pallbearer.

I leapt out of the car and made my way in a fast walk towards the hearse, relieved that the coffin was still inside. Kelsey appeared beside me.

"Oh shit, this is really real," Kelsey said.

I slowed down and turned to hug her. Her face mask was down below her nose, I pinched the mouth part and lifted it up on her face.

"I got you," I repeated the words said to me from Joseph earlier.

Kelsey looked up at me, her tear-soaked face bunched up. "I just want this day to be over," she muttered.

The six of us assumed our positions at the end of the vehicle to accept the coffin. As it slid out we all helped each other. We didn't raise it to our shoulders, but walked with it at hip level, grasping the thick, gold handles. Following the direction of the assistant again.

We carried the coffin through the headstones towards the frame that was laying partially on a freshly dug grave and gently placed it in the designated spot. The mound of earth covered in green astro turf fabric, to the side. The newly etched gravestone lined up perfectly with the cut lines of the hole in the earth.

Robert Alfred Lavoie
1973-2021

'And until we meet again my son,
may God hold you in the hollow of his hands'

I drifted back through the crowd. I looked and found Joseph. He was standing by a headstone, a short distance from the cars, and Anthony was standing near him.

Joseph smiled at me. He took my hand. We turned together.

"We thank all of you for coming out here today, but remind you that we need to practise social distancing," the priest announced to the crowd. The funeral director and his assistant set up a tripod with a cellphone pointed at the grave.

"Again if you have family unable to attend, please now direct them to the link provided by Mr. and Mrs. Lavoie," the priest said.

A few moments passed, the director gave a thumbs up to the priest.

Everyone was spaced out evenly across the graveyard. Joseph and I stood adjacent to the tripod, where the funeral director busied himself with the broadcasting, and the cemetery workers positioned the coffin over the grave.

The priest emptied a small flask of holy water onto the coffin, as he started about his final prayers.

The two cemetery workers, dressed in thick yard clothes, started the silent mechanism to lower the coffin partially into the grave.

Kelsey appeared in front of me, holding a bouquet of pink and white roses. She handed one to me, one to Joseph, one to Anthony and moved to the next cluster of people.

One by one we approached the coffin, laying our roses on top. I felt a strange sense of closure. A sense of ending. Someone that I had once loved, spent a large portion of my life with, was laying in the wooden box, now partially submerged in the ground.

I returned to where I had been standing, passing Martha and Alfred, whose eyes looked spent. They stood clutching each other.

Without another word, the cemetery workers moved towards the frame holding up the coffin. It started to lower into the ground. A few long moments passed. The flat ropes holding the coffin became slack. The lowering was complete.

The priest finished his sermon.

With Martha and Alfred leading, the crowd slowly made its way back towards the cars.

Anthony appeared at my side. His eyes were red from crying.

"Ok, well... Guess we should press on to Kels's," Anthony said.

We moved back towards the car. Anthony moving to the driver's seat, Joseph guided me to the front passenger seat and sat behind me in the back of the car.

We waited for a few moments as people returned to their cars, one by one. We all made our way out of the cemetery and out into the regularity of a Sunday morning in Montreal.

"That was beautiful," Anthony said, as we joined the other cars on the highway.

I had nothing to say.

Our car pulled away, transporting us from the small space that existed in the collective grief that only happens at funerals We continued up the highway towards Montreal.

My phone buzzed. It was Kelsey. 'You are coming to my place right?'

'Yes,' I replied.

"Why don't we drop you off at Kelsey's place and we will walk over without the car?" Joseph said from the back seat.

"What? I mean, sure... there are going to be people I have to talk to, but it won't take that long," I replied.

"Yeah, but I think maybe Kelsey wants to talk to you without us around," Joseph finished.

"Yeah, ok," I replied tiredly. I wanted this day to be over sooner than it was.

We drove in silence the small distance to Kelsey's home.

Anthony stopped the car in the alleyway. "Ok, we will see you in about half an hour," Anthony said as I stepped out of the car. I nodded back to him, winking at Joseph as I shut the car door.

I made the small walk up the alley to Kelsey's back garden. Kelsey was standing with some friends of hers I did not recognize. I walked up to them. Kelsey had clearly been crying.

"Hey, thanks for coming," Kelsey said. I nodded back at her. I heard the backdoor of the house opening behind me and turned around to see Susan. I had not had a chance to speak to her during any of the services. Susan and I used to get along well, but we hadn't spoken for around two years.

"Hi, how are you?" I asked as she approached me, her stare becoming wider.

"Kelsey, what is he doing here?" she said, turning to Kelsey.

THE DETERMINIST

There was silence in the back garden.

"Robert told me what you did to him, everything you put him through. You should be ashamed of yourself being here today," Susan said, her face becoming redder and redder as she spoke. "You may have fooled everyone else, but I see you for what you are, if you hadn't left him like you did he would still be here," she finished.

I stood, suddenly unable to talk. Kelsey took Susan by the hand and tried to lead her back into the house. "No, I know what I am doing, he shouldn't be here that gay little shit" Susan protested, trying to tear her hand away. "Just get away from my family!" Susan shouted at me, Kelsey holding her by both arms.

I turned and started walking towards the alley.

"Greg!" Kelsey called out. But I kept walking. I made it to the alleyway and out of sight.

I heard footsteps behind me, I didn't turn. I was crying too hard. "Greg, I am so sorry, she is a fucking nightmare. You know she is crazy, right? No one thinks that. No one thinks you shouldn't be here," Kelsey called out to me as she caught up.

"No one knows what he did to me Kels," I said to Kelsey. "It was painful what he did. He toyed with me for years and eventually threw me away. He was always cheating... Always withholding... and now, he goes and fucking dies, and I have to grieve this all over again... I hate him for dying," I stopped myself from saying more with a hand over my mouth.

Kelsey put her hands on my shoulders and pulled me into a hug. "I know," she said with a sob. "I know. I knew because he did things like that to people before you. I know. I love him, he was my brother, but he was complex," Kelsey was crying. "I am so sorry," she continued.

"I have to go. I have to go get some stuff, I leave tomorrow. Take care Kelsey," I said with as much of a final tone I could muster. Kelsey resisted my attempt to pull away from her. We stood in the mid-afternoon chill, clutching each other and crying. Kelsey began to talk. "He wasn't the best, but-" she stated.

"You know, it wouldn't have been so bad if he had just been better to me over the last few years," I said, still crying. "I will always love him, and I will never forgive him," I concluded.

Kelsey let out another sob.

"Come and see me for a coffee tomorrow morning before you go, please?" Kelsey requested. I nodded and started turning away from her. I heard as she started to sob and walk back to her garden of mourners.

Walking down the alleyway I pulled out my cell phone to text Joseph.

'Leaving Kelsey's now. Will be back in 15."

I started the walk through downtown Montreal. Still wearing the suit. Still crying. The streets were quiet. The sky was still a brilliant blue.

CHAPTER 16

I was in water. I looked up and saw mangrove roots lining a bank of earth. I swam up and climbed up the mangrove roots, they were six feet tall and difficult to climb, but I made it. There was a small nook where I could rest while climbing.

When I got up, there were people on a beach, everyone was happy and fit, and tan. I looked down at my body. In comparison, I looked bloated and pale.

As I made my way along the beach, I saw a man running towards me, waving to me. He was my height, fit and lean with exceptional abs.

He approached me with a smile and started talking about the lockdowns, "do you think the gyms will be open soon?" he asked. I didn't respond.
We walked past an old, very 70's era looking gym with mainly cardio equipment inside. It was padlocked, but you could climb through the window to get inside. We didn't enter, he led me away from it, further down the beach.

"I just need the gyms to be open, to have the ritual of moving my body," he said. "Especially the year I am having, I can't find myself anymore," he said looking at me with bewilderment.

He reached down and picked up a banana that was on the beach. He broke it in half without peeling it. He passed the top half to me.

"These are good, I like the nutty flavour," he said.

I bit into my end of the banana, with the skin on. The inside reminded me of hazelnuts. I looked at it, wondering what it was.

We kept walking, it was dusk at the beach. He turned to me as we passed a group of people watching two men fight. They were brutally fist fighting. The sound of knuckles on skin, a crowd leering them on.

"Yeah, they are going to stop someday. Then it will be our turn," he said to me with a cheery expression.

***

My therapist had another new hairstyle. Very severe lines cutting down the front of her face. It suited her new glasses. She had recently moved to Nova Scotia, where there were fewer Covid restrictions. The move also solidified the fact that therapy would now be completely online.

"So, this man, do you recognize him?" she asked

"No, I don't. Like, I cannot put a name on him but I know his face, like, he seems familiar, but a total stranger," I replied.

"Hmm. I just wonder, did this beach setting feel familiar?" she asked.

"Yeah, well I have had a few dreams in this place, the beach place is always somewhere I end up in my dreams, after a while..." I replied.

"How do you feel about the gyms being closed still?" she asked.

"It sucks, it's shit and I don't like it. Nothing I can really do though," I replied.

"Hmm, well, I am not sure what this dream means. Why don't we go over some of what happened over the last week," she said.

"Pretty regular lockdown week to be honest. Joseph has been great, we really hit a curve there. I thought he was going to leave me after Montreal, but we talked things out. He comes over most mornings to do yoga with me before work. Things are good." I replied.

"What happened with Joseph in Montreal?" she asked.

"Well, it is a lot to go through, I couldn't imagine what it must have been like for him. Watching your boyfriend put his ex's coffin in the ground, he saw Robert's family before meeting mine, or me meeting his," I replied.

"Well, I think it speaks to you as a person Greg, he loves you and wants to be with you," she said sweetly.

"I mean, maybe, yeah. I just cannot think of what this would have been like without him. Or without Caroline, or Anthony. It's all been so much, like, too much," I replied, absentmindedly saying the things that you are supposed to say in therapy. I picked up a pencil that was next to my laptop and fiddled with it, twirling it through my fingers.

"You sound a little distracted, is everything ok?" she asked, I felt a small panic, I had been caught phoning it in.

"I just... I sometimes feel a little nihilistic about all of this. I mean the whole thing, life," I said, with an exacerbated tone.

"Well, it is understandable that after the sudden death of someone from your past, you might have these feelings, it is important to remember that you have surrounded yourself with good people," she replied.

"Yeah but that's just it. What if they surrounded themselves with me? What if we are all just in each other's lives because that's how things end up? Like it's all just pre-aligned? It feels so trapping sometimes. Claustrophobic," I said.

"You feel as though you don't have control over what happens to you?" she asked.

"No, well, I know I do, but fuck me, all I have done for the last few years is react to things. Robert was horrible to me, and I reacted by building a better life for myself, then he died. The pandemic happened and I reacted by filling my days with small tasks. I was lonely and I started dating and that worked out great. I met someone amazing, but it's all just reactions. Things just happen and I react." I could feel myself getting upset. "I... just... sorry, I just get so frustrated thinking that I never truly make something for myself because it was the way I planned it," I continued, starting to hear the hoarseness in my voice.

"Do you think you didn't plan on having relationships? It's not like you were told to meet these people, you sought them out," she concluded.

"Yeah, but it just feels so futile. Like inevitably Joseph will want to leave me, and I don't know what I can plan to do to stop that from happening," I said, sounding defeated.

"Look, people grow and change. If your relationship with Joseph doesn't last, because it doesn't work, then that is ok. You will have done nothing wrong. Just remember you fell in love with him for who he was, and he fell in love with you for who you are, and you are building a relationship based on that," she said.

I took a long breath in.

I could feel a shift in my mood. "Who do you think the two men fighting in that dream represent?" I asked.

"It's hard to say. They could be parts of you that are going to always be battling, or it could be that unquiet part of you. The reason you do just react sometimes. Remember though, in the dream, there were people surrounding the two men fighting. People had stopped to watch them." she replied. I stared blankly at the screen, blankly into her, hoping she would elaborate.

"What I think this represents is the struggle that we all have in us. It is just gaining more of a literal translation to you. If you have that dream again, or you see those men fighting in your dreams, you can always go up and ask them what they are fighting about," she continued.

I looked at her skeptically. "Like, just walk up and ask them? Won't my subconscious tell me anything it wants in a dream?" I said.

"No, you should be asking questions. The answers are often held by parts of your unconscious. The fact that you saw some violent people fighting is interesting. Everything that happened in a dream, every character is a part of your own unconscious, your shadow self. There is a show of bravado there... Two parts of yourself in a conflict so deep that it has become violent," she finished.

"This makes sense," I said defeatedly. "I sometimes wonder what we are doing here in therapy, then stuff like that comes up," I said.

"Thank you for being honest, sometimes the whole picture won't make sense until we talk about it," she replied.

***

Our session ended the same way most of them did. A cordial goodbye and confirmation email of payment and next scheduled appointment.

I moved to the couch and sat down, taking in what had just been said.

My phone buzzed, it was a text from my mum. 'Good time for a chat?'

I stood up and made my way into the kitchen, poured a glass of white wine and called my mother.

"Hey, Mum, what's up?" I said.

"Oh just checking in to see how you are, Caroline mentioned you had therapy tonight, just wanted to see if you are ok," she said. I was slightly annoyed that Caroline had told her about the session, but it was a small annoyance.

"Oh, yeah, pretty routine, just working through the problems," I said with a small chuckle. "How are you?" I pivoted.

"You know, there is something that they won't tell you in therapy," she said.

"Oh, what's that?" I said with a cheeky tone to my voice.

My mum chuckled. "Well, they will never just tell you that sometimes things happen, like what happened to you over the last year, and it's no one's fault. No one is to blame. It is just things that happen because they have to, and they are terrible," she finished. Her words lingering with me for a moment as I made sense of how profound what she had said was.

"Well actually, my therapist says it's all your fault mum," I said with a serious tone.

"What?" she said quickly.

"Just kidding Mum, I appreciate that. I know that it is a bad time," I said, with another chuckle to my tone.

"I called Martha and Alfred not long after you left Montreal," she said.

I sat up on the couch, every alarm bell ringing in my head. "What did you say to them? How did you get their number?" I asked, trying not to sound panicked.

"I looked them up on the internet. I called to give them my condolences and told them about how Robert was such a good addition to our family when the two of you were together," she finished.

I paused for a minute.

"Well, that is very nice of you, they would have liked that. But Mum, didn't you hate Robert?" I asked, almost laughing.

"Oh of course I did, the way he broke you, broke my son. No, of course I despised him for what he did, but I would never *not* call a grieving mother to offer some nice words, even if they are total bullshit," she finished.

I sat back and picked up my glass of wine, taking a sip.

"Well, that was nice of you," I said.

"It's good to hear you laughing darling. I really worry about you with the year you are having. It's not easy, and I don't really know how you, well... I am just proud of you Greg. It must have been so difficult to go through that," she finished.

"Yeah, it has been hard. But it should get easier soon. The worst of it is that it feels like he dumped me all over again. I sit on this couch and think about all the times we sat on this couch together. And my apartment is full of stuff that was ours because we split everything up. And now it is truly the only thing that I will ever have to remind me of the good times, and the bad times," I said. "Sorry, I am rambling on," I finished.

"No no, speak darling. Remember, no matter how it ended, you did have a good relationship at some point with him, and then it was bad. And you put yourself back together without him. You spent time alone, then you met someone new, and fell in love. That is all normal in life. What is truly tragic is that he died. He cannot exist in your life in any other way now. You won't get closure, but you just keep moving on, one foot in front of the other darling, with your chin up," she said.

I felt a small tear roll down my cheek. I was not used to my mother being so profound and poignant. It was like talking to the person she was to other people. She used to have so many friends that would come to her for advice, but never take it herself.

"Thanks Mum," I said.

"I love you darling," she replied.

"I love you too, thanks for calling. I just gotta get going with some stuff around here. I'll give you a call around this time next week?" I said.

THE DETERMINIST

We said our goodbyes and I sat alone on my couch, with my glass of wine, completely dumbfounded by the conversation.

I stepped out onto the street in front of my apartment building. It was a balmy spring night in Toronto, humid but comfortable. The sun was setting. I walked down my street and out onto the main road. All the other evening walkers were out, in their short sleeves and facemasks. There was a buzz in the air. I walked past the park and along the road to the house that Robert and I had shared.

There was a 'For Rent' sign in the planter box in the front door.

I looked up at the house, to the top floor. The deck furniture I had made years ago was still on the balcony. Part of me wanted to go up and retrieve it. I don't have any need or want for it though.

I looked into the flower bed lining the side of the house and saw all the little bulb heads peeking up, getting ready for the spring bloom. The daffodils I had planted when we moved in were just about to start flowering. I took a step back from the sidewalk and out to the road. Looking up at the house. Taking in a moment before leaving. So much history in those walls.

I turned on my heels and started walking down the sidewalk, past the intersection, and out onto the busy Toronto street.

Printed by Libri Plureos GmbH in Hamburg, Germany